SHYLOCK IS SHAKESPEARE

SHYLOCK IS SHAKESPEARE

Kenneth Gross

The University of Chicago Press
Chicago & London

KENNETH GROSS is professor of English at the University of Rochester. He is the author of *Spenserian Poetics: Idolatry, Iconoclasm, and Magic* (1985), *The Dream of the Moving Statue* (1992, reprinted in 2006), and, most recently, *Shakespeare's Noise* (2001), published by the University of Chicago Press.

The University of Chicago Press, Chicago 60637
The University of Chicago Press, Ltd., London
© 2006 by The University of Chicago
All rights reserved. Published 2006
Printed in the United States of America

15 14 13 12 11 10 09 08 07 06   1 2 3 4 5

ISBN-13: 978-0-226-30977-4 (cloth)
ISBN-10: 0-226-30977-0 (cloth)

Library of Congress Cataloging-in-Publication Data
Gross, Kenneth.
Shylock is Shakespeare / Kenneth Gross.
    p. cm.
Includes bibliographical references (p.   ) and index.
ISBN 0-226-30977-0 (alk. paper)
1. Shakespeare, William, 1564–1616. Merchant of Venice. 2. Shakespeare, William, 1564–1616—Characters—Shylock. 3. Shylock (Fictitious character) I. Title.
PR2825.G763 2006
822.3'3—dc22

                    2005032150

∞ The paper used in this publication meets the minimum requirements of the American National Standard for Information Sciences—Permanence of Paper for Printed Library Materials, ANSI Z39.48-1992.

FOR

Angus Fletcher

Contents

Preface

This book is an essay on Shylock's singularity. It returns to the perennial strangeness of his life and presence in *The Merchant of Venice*, his opacity as a dramatic character. It examines how he organizes around himself the energy of the play even as he throws it off balance, shattering its generic clarity. Shylock has an atomic quality, compact yet explosive. His power lies in an emerging isolation of purpose and person—what he will call his "bond"—and in his refusal to be answerable to the ordinary terms of law or reason, at the same time as he makes the law his own. It lies also in an idiosyncratic eloquence that at once exposes and occults Shylock's inner life, even as his words show the world a mirror of its hidden rage. This eloquence has its darkly comic as well as its tragic aspects. His character embodies what you might call a poetics of repugnancy. There is something in Shylock that resists absorption or clarification. He is like a Möbius strip, his inside and outside continually turning into one another.

Shylock's ferocious idiosyncrasy makes a strange place for *The Merchant of Venice* within the Shakespearean canon as a whole. In the play, a character intended as one piece of a larger dramatic machine so draws the poet's attention that he gains a life that threatens to dominate or deform the whole. If this begins as an accident, it leads to a genuine breakthrough, and after Shylock something in the plays is different. He looks forward to many aspects of the later plays—the wild interiority of the tragedies, for one thing, and their way of rooting into reality, private and public, through staging voices of rage—even as he remains a thing apart. John Berryman found a striking way to represent the discovery. He said that in Shylock Shakespeare first "tasted blood." The metaphor suggests that Shakespeare is a hunting dog whose more predatory instincts suddenly find their proper object; or he is a creature who in tasting blood threatens to slip out of his domesticated role, his appetites reverting to a hunger for something more primal. The blood Shakespeare tasted would be, if I read Berryman rightly, both the blood of the audience and the blood of a character, or both together, their hearts' blood. The blood that Shakespeare tasted was also his own. That is one reason why we can still taste it. One source of Shylock's interest is that he composes a powerful yet covert double for Shakespeare. Shylock's singularity translates Shakespeare's singularity, which includes his chameleon-like capacity for disguise and his fascination with extremes of ambiguity, his ability to transmute pain and pleasure, his skill in marrying the general and the particular, and his ruthless way with audiences. Even as I describe Shylock's life in the play itself, I have attempted to evoke this shadowy identification, to give it imaginative force. The very name Shylock will claim us more strongly if we hear in it a hidden, echoic double of the name Shakespeare.

Related to these questions is another one, the issue of Shylock's complex afterlife in performance, fiction, and criticism, as well as in the language of antisemitic cliché. This afterlife—what John Gross calls Shylock's "legacy," his deed of gift—is more extensive than that of any other character in Shakespeare's plays, save perhaps Hamlet, and even Hamlet cannot rival Shylock's chilling passage into the commonplace. I take up this matter primarily in discussing fictions by Heinrich Heine, Ludwig Lewisohn, and Philip Roth, and more briefly in remarks on Jorge Luis Borges and Marcel Proust. At their best, such writers turn us back to the riddle at the heart of the original play, even as they open it up to fresh literary, philosophical, and historical associations. One part of that riddle lies in Shylock's being a creature of antisemitic slander and one who transforms that slander, both resisting its misconceptions and tapping its rhetorical and psychic energies, playing with its violence, making that abuse serve him as mask and mouthpiece. His way of surviving in his world says something about how the character survives in history. The old question of what kind of human density Shakespeare has lent to Shylock remains inescapable. What we need is to see how the current of abuse becomes itself a tool for Shylock, one source of his intenser dramatic life, and part of what, ironically, humanizes him.

There are many friends to whom I am indebted in this book for their help and encouragement. Daniel Albright, Genevieve Guenther, John Hollander, James Longenbach, Herbert Marks, and Joanna Scott read the manuscript with probing eyes, letting me see better its shape and possibilities. An array of conversations with Tom Bishop, Harold Bloom, Soelve Curdts, Lawrence Danson, Richard Howard, George Kateb, U. C. Knoepflmacher, Christopher Ricks, Esther Schor, Nigel Smith, Adam Sutcliffe, Gordon Teskey, Rosanna Warren, and Froma Zeitlin led me to vital discoveries. As always, my students have surprised me with thoughts that made the play more surprising. I would like to thank my editor at the University of Chicago Press, Alan Thomas, and Erik Carlson, my copy editor. My deepest debt is to Angus Fletcher, who kept urging me to focus on the plainest questions, even as our conversations showed me so many doors to be opened, so many tracks to be pursued in the labyrinth of Shakespeare's play.

A Note on Texts

All quotations from *The Merchant of Venice* are taken from the New Cambridge Shakespeare text, edited by M. M. Mahood (Cambridge: Cambridge University Press, 1987). Quotations from all other plays and poems of Shakespeare are from *The Riverside Shakespeare*, ed. G. Blakemore Evans, 2d ed. (Boston: Houghton Mifflin, 1997). Unless otherwise noted, all biblical quotations are taken from the Geneva translation (1560).

Chapter One

BEGINNING

If after the trial of Antonio I found myself walking with Shylock through some narrow street or *calle* in Venice (I say walking because I cannot imagine Shylock in a gondola), I would ask him the question that always hits me after reading or watching the trial scene: What could you have been thinking? Given what you know of Venetian society, polity, and law, and of the Venetians' very particular malice toward you, what made you suppose that you would be allowed to take the life of a Christian merchant in open court? How could you think that you would be allowed to execute your mad bond, cut into Antonio's flesh, and not only that, but in the process put so nakedly on display the Venetian law's impotence to save its own—indeed, its exquisitely adjusted power to abet you in your revenge? Recall how Shylock in this scene seems able to creep inside and become himself the vengeful spirit of his enemies' laws, reanimating Venetian law for the purpose of murder rather than justice, profit, or order, stealing for himself the law's necessary, often concealed violence. How did he imagine he could survive the exposure of his own rage and contempt, which includes his contempt for the contempt that others have so regularly heaped upon him? He gives and hazards all the rage he has. He is the very

I

spirit of hazard, even as he masters the scene. He makes himself an open wound onstage. He may surprise even himself in forcing into the open what is hidden, making out of his claim on the bond the fresh vehicle of an old anger, even if the sources and objects of that anger remain difficult to fix. I suppose you might say Shylock is confident that he will win his case, knowing how devoted the Venetians are to the laws that guard their economic power. But it is still a wild gamble, the wildest gamble in this play about fortune. In this scene Shylock puts the law to use but also shames the law and its upholders, those whom the law itself upholds. He strips the laws bare as he strips himself bare. The trial of Antonio—which quickly turns into the trial of Shylock—is for him what Wallace Stevens calls "the accomplishment of an extremist in an exercise." It is as if King Lear, raging in the storm, were actually allowed to stage the demented trial of his cruel daughters, allowed to anatomize them before a court of madmen and fools, to cut open Regan's chest to see if there is "any cause in nature that make these hard hearts." In *The Merchant of Venice*, Shylock anatomizes his own heart as well as seeking Antonio's. We do not know for sure what he wants to get back, or what he wants the pursuit of his bond's forfeit to yield him. Shylock's is a self-destructive project; it strips him of his living, if not his life. Yet it is a project that gains for him the impression of an interior life, a thinking, more unfathomable and harrowing than that of any other character in the play. It lends him an eloquence that is unaccountable both in its power and in its ordinariness. We start to see what William Hazlitt called the "hard, impenetrable, dark groundwork of the character of Shylock."

The Merchant of Venice is a hyperstructured play, as Angus Fletcher once characterized it, preoccupied by wills, boxes, bonds, and rituals of choice and law, not to mention the larger generic structures of the comic fiction. Shylock is at once the exploiter and the victim of such structures. He slips past them even as he makes us feel both their weight and their arbitrariness. This comes through in the way he both feeds and shatters the balance of the comedy. It comes through in how he makes a legal bond such a radical mark of his identity, a vehicle for his rage, even as it drives any more normative notion of legal bonding into the wilderness. These are aspects of what I have come to think of as Shylock's singularity, his particularity or power of idiosyncrasy. *The Merchant of Venice* is Shylock's play, he gives it its point, even as he is larger than the world which tries to contain him. Do the other characters even know what they hate in Shylock? At times one gets the sense that Shylock is invisible to them, that they are accusing a specter, even as he represents something at the core of things as they are. Shylock can seem like a king in exile or disguise. (It is paradoxes such as these that distinguish the originality of Shylock from that of another, perhaps earlier example of Shakespeare's emerging powers of dramatic individuation, the bastard Faulconbridge in *King John*, who for all his improvisatory verve, even a kind of royal spirit, does not shift the axis of the play around himself so sharply, or show anything like Shylock's power to wound.)

Shylock's singularity is bound up with a complex sort of typicality, a typicality that is both a burden and a curse. One aspect of Shylock's exemplary force lies in what he tells us about theater, how he draws on theater's primal energy of role playing, its way of holding up a mirror to those who watch and listen. He attracts attention to himself and manipulates it. He pushes to the limit theater's powers of exposure and concealment, its abiding interest in forms of human shame and shamelessness; he reminds us of the power of the stage to assault its auditors and fetch up impulses otherwise unknown, unacknowledged, and neglected. Shylock's rages speak to Shakespeare's perennial challenge to his audience. Shylock is a man willing, in his own words, to "offend, himself being offended," which means being willing to offend himself. His dramatic authority, his gift to later actors, indeed lies in his power to extend the realm of what is possible onstage, to turn even offense into a complex mystery. This is what makes Shylock so difficult and so enlivening a part to perform onstage. It's clear that many of the great eighteenth- and nineteenth-century actors who humanized the role—men such as Charles Macklin, William Charles Macready, Edmund Kean, and Henry Irving—were drawn to it less out of sympathy for Jews than because it gave them an occasion for reinventing the scope of their own acting, calling up an energy of performance, a mode of animation, more challenging, true, and electric than what their audiences had become accustomed to. Thinking about what can be played in Shylock also helps us think about what may be unplayable in Shylock—for if this is a threshold play, it is partly because here Shakespeare places at the center of his dramatic script a point of stark resistance to performance.

The power of the character also lies in what he reveals in more general terms about the human enigma, its jointure of freedom and dependence, secrecy and histrionics, alienness and complicity, its capacity for terror, for aggression and resentment, for giving itself over to the inhuman. The play explores what it means to inhabit this enigma, this divisive jointure, to expand it from within and force it into new combinations. Whatever is shown in Shylock strikes us more strongly given his stark isolation, and not just from his family or the society of Venice. G. Wilson Knight observes forcefully that while Shylock in his solitary rages mirrors the riven consciousnesses of Shakespeare's great tragic heroes, unlike theirs, his protests find no echo or matrix in a larger cosmos, in the anger of ghosts, the babble of madmen, the guilty murmurings of sleepwalkers, military and civic violence, or the chaos of the weather. Shylock is never visible, as Hamlet, Lear, Macbeth, and others are, to the world of the dead or the world of dream. It is such surrounding forces that both sustain and expand the words and consciousness of these tragic figures, that give them their breadth of relation, their diffuse generality. These influences make each of the tragic characters "an inalienable part of the universal structure" framed in their plays, linking them further to a hidden, Dionysiac principle, or what Knight, quoting W. B. Yeats, calls "a fabulous, formless darkness." Their part in a larger tragic matrix helps to save these characters from such humiliation as Shylock suffers. "The great tragedies are metaphysical explorations of that which lies behind, or within, the human enigma; Shylock is a study drawn more directly from that enigma, from life itself as we know it." This is perhaps why, as Fletcher suggests, Shylock's eloquence is of a different order; it is less an eloquence of consciousness than "an eloquence of being."

Shylock's isolation as character also mirrors Shakespeare's isolation as author, his sense of what the audience cannot know about his fictions and what drives them. The importance of Shylock lies in what he reveals about the Shakespearean enigma as much as the human enigma. Shylock provides us a mirror of Shakespeare's sense of himself as a human author, as a creator of artifacts for the stage, and of his violence against those creations. We can see in Shylock's situation Shakespeare's comment on the risks entailed by his making, his joining together of exposure and deep self-concealment, his wounded and wounding generosity, and the costs of that generosity. Shylock shows us the vexed conditions of the playwright's success, in particular as he reflects something about Shakespeare's uncertain bond with his audience, the world that eats his children by eye and ear, a world on which Shakespeare takes his own kind of revenge. Shylock's rage is Shakespeare's rage, which includes, most centrally, the rage of Shakespeare the dramatic artist. In this he provides as powerful a clue to Shakespeare's artistic impulses as the characters of Hamlet, Falstaff, and Prospero. What *The Merchant of Venice* tells us about its author may be all the sharper given the play's awkward, imperfect shape as a theatrical artifact. As R. P. Blackmur noted in regard to certain texts of Henry James (for example, *The Sacred Fount*), "It is often in his relative failures that an artist's drive is most clearly defined; if only because in his purest successes there is the sense of the self-born, self-driven, and self-complete and these qualities escape definition."

Something in the composition of Shylock has made it possible for him to survive, to possess a literary and theatrical afterlife of peculiar vividness and complexity. The grounds and quality of that survival—the question of how we remember Shylock—are also part of what I want to explore in this book. To some degree this survival depends on his conflicted position in the play itself. For all the power with which he claims our attention, Shylock at the end of the play is radically incomplete, denied a part in any fully realized action. This is something reinforced by the very artful cruelty with which the trial scene ends, leaving Shylock so quickly undone, stripped of legal claims, voiceless, compelled to become a Christian under threat of death. The forced conversion is Shakespeare's most conspicuous addition to the traditional pound-of-flesh legend. But the idea of assimilating him within a Christian community only makes his isolation more complex; Shylock at the end has no part in a clear political, social, or spiritual faction. He steps into a void and is almost forgotten by the play itself, which continues on for another act. This incompleteness is part of what keeps us guessing at this character; he stays alive because we can neither quite let him go nor decide what form to give him in our minds.

If it is Shylock's incompleteness that keeps him vivid, he also survives through time by virtue of being too complete. His very isolation within the system of the play reinforces this. Cut off from a larger world of relation, Shylock stays around not just as a scarily open question—a wound drawing in fresh care and violence—but as a closed, blank cliché. He survives the way a stereotype survives, a falsely simple, self-defining truth, despite his own attempts in the play to shatter this, or at least to put it to shattering uses. The diffused image of Shylock as "the figure of *the hated man*," as the actor Abraham Morevski called him—a version of the cruel, cunning, divisive, abject, legalistic, and treacherous Jew—points to his more troubling gift to history. It is through Shylock's becoming part of history, part of the language of European antisemitism, part of what both Jews and Christians know and do not know about Jews, that he feels unlike any other Shakespearean character. Shylock's face, his words, in some cases his bare name, live a compulsive, shadowy life in our history and its conversations, always ready to emerge from the background, continuously woven into other forms of monstrous rumor or cunning lie, sustaining them, helping to enlarge their scope. Shylock is a form of knowledge as well as a lie, not just shorthand for moneylender or Jew, but a name for a way of being, a certain relation to the past.

Marcel Proust shows us one form of Shylock's ambiguous presence in a scene from *Time Regained* (1927), the last volume of *In Search of Lost Time*. Here the narrator comes across his school friend Albert Bloch at a grand party given by the Princesse de Guermantes. It is the occasion when Marcel grasps the possibility of dedicating himself to the great novel he has always deferred writing, the moment when he starts to see the shaping power of time itself, the strange gulfs time opens up and the eerie filiations it lays bare. At the party, Bloch, always a decidedly secular Jew, appears transformed. He is now elegant, charming, distinguished, and much sought after; he has shed his old vulgarity and self-consciousness, not to mention his mask of genial antisemitism, which the young Marcel had witnessed at Balbec. He has taken a new name, Jacques du Rozier. His very body has undergone a metamorphosis, his once curly hair is flattened, his moustache "suppressed," and the Jewish curve of his nose now "scarcely more visible than is the deformity of a hunchbacked woman who skillfully arranges her appearance." Yet at this party where the narrator sees so many ghosts, Bloch too is haunted. At one moment, when Bloch comes "bounding into the room like a hyena," Marcel sees a man closer to death, still desperate about his place in the world, closer to his anxious, beloved father than he could bear to know:

What did this profit him? At close quarters, in the translucency of a face in which, at a greater distance or in a bad light, I saw only youthful gaiety (whether because it survived there or because I with my recollections evoked it), I could detect another face, almost frightening, racked with anxiety, the face of an old Shylock, waiting in the wings, with his make-up prepared, for the moment when he would make his entry on to the stage and already reciting his first line under his breath.

Elsewhere in his novel Proust speaks about the troubled place of Jews in French society, evoking their powers of survival—at once social and historical—their sense of persecution and deep capacity for loyalty. Among assimilated Jews he acknowledges a fearful secrecy and solitude, a power to know each other by mysterious affiliation combined with a need to shun each other's company, even to seek out for friends those who most hate them, all of which mark their hidden ties with the other "cursed race" of homosexuals. The name of Shylock is invoked in the above passage to fix the narrator's perception of some hidden truth about his friend, a truth that makes itself visible despite the self-conscious disguise. Yet one cannot quite tell if it is some essential Jewishness that is marked by recourse to the old label or an acknowledgement that this form of Jewishness is after all itself a disguise, another mask that knows itself to be a mask, waiting in the wings to supplant another performance. (Is it an unconscious acknowledgement of his lineage that Bloch's assumed name evokes the principal street of the old Jewish quarter of Paris, the rue des Rosiers?)

As Proust's text makes clear, it is not just that there are different versions of Shylock in our memory, it is that there are different kinds remembrance at work, different ways of remembering the character. We could divide them crudely into two species. One form of memory is more individuated, attached to the particulars of the play itself and its performances, holding on to Shylock in his theatrical context, however ambiguously he is perceived. Here we know him as a dramatic character. The other form of memory is more schematic and diffused, yet no less tenacious, and more fully bound up with a forgetting of the play, a forgetting to which the play itself contributes. In the latter case the mere name Shylock takes on a life of its own, cut off from any necessary knowledge of its origin (as happens also with the phrase "a pound of flesh").

These different species of memory, in all their varying incarnations and degrees, play against each other in the text's afterlife. They shadow each other, so that the character of Shylock appears always variously fragmented, refracted, distorted, or emptied out, a ghost of himself, yet still curiously potent—a movement that, as Richard Halpern has shown, is at work in modernist images of the Jew more generally. In texts like the one I've quoted from Proust, it is hard to measure just which sort of memory is most powerful.

It is this ambiguity in how we remember Shylock, as much as the play's taint of antisemitism, that accounts for something in Shylock's afterlife that I otherwise find mysterious. This is the fact that it is hard to find in modern poetry, fiction, or drama a truly canonical reimagining of Shakespeare's Shylock, one that stays true to the force of the original character even as it seeks to create something new. There is nothing to compare, say, to the way that Luigi Pirandello reinvents the figure of Hamlet, the pretend madman, in his great play *Henry IV*, or to the way that Samuel Beckett's Hamm, the haunted son and abusive father of *Endgame*, gives us a stark revision of Hamlet and King Lear at once. There is no poetic retelling of *The Merchant of Venice* to compare with W. H. Auden's *Sea and the Mirror*, a book that finds voices for characters in *The Tempest* that open them up to fresh moral and poetic recognitions. Shylock continues to haunt modern authors, both Jewish and non-Jewish, and the play itself has never ceased being performed and studied, inflected and reinflected. But when it comes to the invention of a new literary character, the face of Shylock, unless it reappears as a grotesque relic or revenant—as in the early poetry of T. S. Eliot—is something that must either be exorcised or go more deeply in disguise, as in the case of James Joyce's Leopold Bloom.

I doubt that Shakespeare, theatrical pragmatist that he was, had much interest in Jews when he started writing, apart from what he could make of them in a dramatic text. In designing *The Merchant of Venice*, he drew on some of the same elements of antisemitic fantasy that fed Christopher Marlowe's *Jew of Malta*; he increased their virulence as well as their ambiguity by making Shylock so much less a puppet than Marlowe's Machiavellian Barabas. Yet how we are to characterize the poet's strategy remains a question. There is much in the text that leads one to call it antisemitic, yet by itself that is too simple. Nor is it useful to say that the play is, as someone suggested to me, prosemitic, though from an aesthetic point of view you might say that it is pro-Shylock. The play refuses—more, it anatomizes—the kind of factionalism of thought that provokes such readings; this is part of its moral and aesthetic power. What continues to compel us in Shylock depends on things that cannot be made sense of strictly in terms of his Jewish identity. Attempts to make Shylock into an emblem of Jewish victimage or Jewish heroism, a creature around which a sense of cultural fate can rally, moving as they are, often fail to see how much the play outrages such an identity. Under the spell of such readings Shylock threatens to become a kind of golem, the artificial man of Kabbalistic tradition and Jewish folklore, a being whose life, for all that it is intended to be redemptive, inevitably causes damage to those who have created him. The fact is that Shylock has to be saved from sectarian readings, whether Jewish or Christian. Or perhaps the idea of saving Shylock has to be given up entirely. (The idea of helping him is a disease that can only be cured by taking to one's bed, as Franz Kafka's Hunter Gracchus says of himself.) Shylock's complexity is such that every approach to making sense of him is itself a trial, a test of our moral and literary tact.

Shakespeare's startling achievement is that whatever we call Shylock's humanity emerges exactly through rather than simply in spite of the shapes of antisemitic abuse that frame his character onstage. It has to do with how Shylock inhabits and makes use of that abuse, how the forms of hatred feed our response to his words, including the face of his inner life. How do we understand the inner life of a slander? How can that life be repossessed by the one slandered? What does Shakespeare thus tell us about the logic of antisemitism? How is the mechanism of hatred also a mechanism

of poetry? *The Merchant of Venice* is a play that explores the drama-
turgy of repugnancy, the aesthetics of things repugnant—taking
the word both in its more commonplace meaning, where it relates
to a feeling of disgust or hatred aroused in us by a person or thing,
and in its older, philosophical usage, referring to something contradictory or inconsistent, unresponsive to logical reasoning. Is there
a specifically Shakespearean repugnancy? And what would that tell
us about a specifically Shakespearean humanity?

Let me end these opening remarks by touching on a telling, if mi-
nor, moment in Shylock's afterlife, one that occurs in a story by
Jorge Luis Borges, "*Deutsches Requiem*," from his 1949 collection *The
Aleph*. This story is narrated by a former commandant of a German
concentration camp. Writing on the eve of his execution by the
Allies, he offers a studied apologia for his life. In particular, he
describes the august purity and heroic sacrifice of self, even of the
insidious emotion of compassion, required of him by his commitment to Nazism. It is an act of will of a sort that has helped, even
in the defeat of Nazism, to ensure the triumph of violence in the
world. He goes on to admit that such purity of faith was once, but
only once, challenged: by his inescapable, humiliating love and
compassion for a Jewish poet named David Jerusalem who was in-
terned in his camp. This love threatened his passion for that ideal
around which he had formed his life. In feeling such an attachment, the commandant tells us, he began to see Jerusalem, at first
his angel—a poet of "meticulous and painstaking love" for ordinary things—as something of a devil. It is a transformation whose
pathological shape even the narrator himself seems to recognize:
"Everything in the world can be the seed of a possible hell; a face,
a word, a compass, an advertisement for cigarettes—anything can
drive a person insane if that person cannot manage to put it out of

his mind. . . . In my eyes, [Jerusalem] was not a man, not even a Jew; he had become a symbol of a detested region of my soul." To have found the will to drive this poet to commit suicide was thus, he says, a triumph over that hell of love in himself.

What most interests me in this account of the origins and spiritual costs of antisemitism is a small detail. The narrator tells us that among David Jerusalem's works is a poem entitled "Rosenkranz Talks with the Angel." It is a versified soliloquy "in which a sixteenth-century London moneylender tries in vain, as he is dying, to exculpate himself, never suspecting that the secret justification for his life is that he has inspired one of his clients (who has seen him only once, and has no memory even of that) to create the character Shylock." We hear nothing more about the poem in Borges's story. Yet this brief moment offers a mirror in which to view the enigma of Shylock and his creation. Borges's imaginary text, first of all, speaks to the fragile origins of a dramatic character. It hints at the contingencies of experience that start such a character in the mind of the poet; it suggests that a mereness or scarcity of acquaintance is for this author preferable to fuller knowledge. ("The historian, essentially, wants more documents than he can really use; the dramatist only wants more liberties than he can really take," writes Henry James.) Borges also touches on the unpredictable acts of will that transmute such accidents of experience, acts that may not even be fully recognized by the artist himself. Shylock begins as a person encountered only for a moment. He has the fragile concreteness of someone met in passing on a crowded street. (Shylock is indeed a creature of the streets, gathering news there, undertaking deals, becoming himself the object of news and mocking rumor.) The moneylender Rosenkranz almost as rapidly disappears into oblivion and yet is transfigured in the very act of being forgotten, a forgetting itself enshrined by the later poet. We are reminded at once of the uncertain grounds of Shylock's gestural life and of its survival in time—in Jerusalem's fantasy the actual person of the moneylender drops from the poet's memory, his afterimage passing to one dramatic character and his mere name to another. Borges's story also joins the elusive origins of a literary character, even of the blessing he provides for the dying man, to the inaccessible origins of human hatred. The story speaks to the ways we create hells within our minds, and of the literal violence by which we may try to banish those hells. David Jerusalem is a mirror of Shylock and Shakespeare both, a mirror of Borges, too, the alchemist of literary memory, a mirror of their vulnerability, their joining of oblivion and survival. Jerusalem, or Jerusalem's Rosenkranz, also gives us a mirror of the story's chilling narrator, a man who himself "tries in vain, as he is dying, to exculpate himself," to find a secret justification for his life in his purity of hatred, as if that hatred were itself a blessing. The whole fiction reminds us of why Shylock, as he survives, is a little dangerous to handle. He is like a piece of fissionable material whose energy is not entirely consumed by the play he fuels. The gamble, the desperate wish of Borges's fiction, is that the work of the artist in creating such a character may become a source of blessing for himself and others, though admittedly a fragile one, all but unknown, and certainly no defense against fanatic violence. If Shylock is a blessing, he is a blessing to struggle with. He is like that wounding creature—no angel, just "some man"—with whom Jacob wrestles at the ford of the Jabbok before returning to his homeland.

Chapter Two

THE HEART OF IT

Who is Shylock? Shylock is Shakespeare. Shylock is Shakespeare and Shakespeare is Shylock. He is not only Antonio's double but Shakespeare's double, his brother and other, a piece of deep dissimulation joined with a startling kind of exposure. The idea edges toward the asymptote of impossibility. Shakespeare always reminds us that hearts are the most shadowy of things.

Start with the names. They both have a similar feel on the tongue and in the ear. There is the same breathy hush of the unvoiced sibilant "sh" that begins each one and the sharp shock of the unvoiced stop "k" at middle or end. The rhythm of both hovers between a trochee and a spondee. Each binds two monosyllabic words, both of Anglo-Saxon derivation. (The name Shylock itself is, as Stephen Orgel has shown, no invention; if it echoes the biblical "Selah" or Shiloh, even the Hebrew *shalakh* [cormorant], it is in fact a name with ancient Saxon roots, meaning white-haired. The Shylocks of sixteenth-century London, Orgel notes, included "goldsmiths, mercers, and most visibly of all, scriveners." So the name might have been no more uncommon to the play's audience than that of its author.) The names show a similar two-step of adjective and noun or verb and noun, shy and shake, lock and spear, a feeling and an action, an opening and something that opens, also kills. What distance do we travel from one syllable to the next? Placed side by side, the names tempt various Joycings: Shakelock and Shyspear, Spysheer and Shapeshock. Lieshock, Slyshock, Sighlack, and Shyblock; Speakshare, Spakehear, Shapekeeper, Shamedseeker, Shadeseer, Shockspeer, and Shockcrier. "Shakespeare" sounds different when caught by the gravitational pull of "Shylock." The fictive name opens up the casket of the historical name, provokes it to dance or dream.

I imagine the playwright himself explaining the connection to us thus:

This character I've made, this Shylock, is myself. He, like me, is a creature of strange commerce, breeding money through what others think of as contaminated, unholy means, trading in a suspect currency that yet seems part of nature, not measurable goods, produce, land, labor, or services, but such odd stuff as words written on sheets of paper and spoken into the air, posturing bodies and souls, the flourishing of old hats, hose, feathers, cloaks, and swords. Like Shylock's, my trade deals with the currency of desire itself, pure and impure, something that is currency and commodity at once; I, like Shylock, deal in strange promises, merry bonds with hidden stings. We both deal in the currency of debt, of wanting. It is not gold and silver but words that I breed as fast as Jacob's ewes. I am, like my moneylender, a master of curious thrifts, a profiteer of loss, building my fortune on illegitimate gains, coining words real and counterfeit, circulating them within a suspect economy. Who knows more than I about trading in and shaping the wants of men, those of my audiences and those of my actors, converting such wants to my own uses? Shylock and I are both professional gamblers, we play with loaded dice, we risk huge sums and insist on carrying out our contracts to the letter. We are both opportunists of reading and speaking, making capital of human weakness, error, and accident, trading in time and hazard. Within our inner ears even the words of abuse that others throw at us—the bestial Jew and the whorish player—can be turned to profit, made into the currency of inner lives. We can both make the dead tongue of the law speak for living, irrational hatreds. And we both create scenes, terrible scenes, dramatic moments that hold up to our audiences a mirror of their own needs, needs they cannot bear to know.

Shylock is I and I am Shylock. The two of us are caught between worlds, between earth and air, matter and spirit. We both feed on shared and secret resources of desire, fear, sorrow, shame, and resentment, thrusting these into sharper and more volatile forms, forms by which we both hide and strip bare our hearts. We thereby take revenge against those whose powers are more literal, who have power to hurt and rarely hold it back. I am content, like Shylock, to offend, myself being offended. I, like Shylock, lay claim to the hearts of my audience, sign with them a contract for a pound of flesh to be cut off from nearest their hearts. As Shylock does, I claim flesh from those who are my doubles, though they do not see how like me they are, as Antonio does not see his own likeness to the Jew. I surprise my hearers with their own hearts. Like Shylock, I want their hearts in exchange for my heart, though it is a heart that I know with as little certainty as they do theirs, a heart that is shadowy, opaque, histrionic, and grotesque, a desert of wounds and a wilderness of monkeys. My heart is a nothing more real than any something, mine own and not mine own, dead and alive at once. For what but his own heart does my Shylock ask when he cries, "I would my daughter were dead at my foot, and the jewels in her ear: would she were hearsed at my foot, and the ducats in her coffin"?

Both Shylock and I make a weapon and a treasure of our wounds, we make of those wounds a magnet to draw in the world. Strange profits hover in the air, ready to rush into such wounds, if one can find the right pain, the right releasing agony. Those wounds find a tongue in our words, a tongue that speaks for others as well as for itself, which is why our words keep both of us from going mad in our solitude. A terrible trade this is. Poor, jealous Robin Greene got it right, remembering my cursing Margaret with her blood-soaked cloth: mine is a tiger's heart wrapped in a player's hide, I am a rebellious puppet set on becoming a puppet master, an upstart crow, an unclean bird that feeds on garbage. A man named Aubrey tells the story that as a boy, learning the profession of butcher, I would kill each calf in great style and afterward make a speech over the corpse. That story is true. The speech was my bond with the creature I killed. My words transfigured the corpse, took its flesh and blood into my mouth, put its death into my speech; I gave people words instead of blood, or words like blood. That is my generosity. I give you meat to eat and dress it well for your devouring, I thus make you innocent of the blood we share. Or, since the audience must be allowed its part in authorship, in murder, I awaken its pitilessness, its desire to make a murder into a sacrifice, an act of justice, even as I toy with its guilt. Think of my Timon and my Titus presiding over their feasts, the one serving his enemy her own children made into pies, the other giving his treacherous friends dishes filled with water for wine and stone for bread. Think of Macbeth, inviting his friends to share a banquet with ghosts.

Like Shylock, I whet my knife, my penknife, on my soul. My father, some time a moneylender, was also a glove-maker, and so I know the life of dead hides, the art by which they are stripped, tanned, stretched, cut, pieced together, and sewn into a second sheathing for the hand. A glove is the hand's mask. And as my Feste says, "A sentence is but a chev'ril glove to a good wit—how quickly the wrong side may be turned outward." Shylock is the glove turned outward.

I feel about myself what I imagine Shylock feeling about himself. Shylock is what I know myself to be. But he is also something in myself that I do not yet know. "Lord, we know what we are, but know not what we may be," says my Ophelia. Shylock is not just myself, but what I might be. Shylock is what I would be if I truly exposed to you what it is my plays cost me, and if I made clear what it is they ask for in return. What I want from you is profit of a fantastic sort, nothing as simple as the return of money for a pleasing spectacle. What I want from you who watch, or want to want, is your heart, both flesh and blood at the same time. I give you my own heart in return, though under a disguise. I give it to those whom I hate for knowing nothing of what it costs me to write as I do. I hate them for not knowing this even as I give them no means to know it. It's something they cannot be allowed to know (though they will take their revenge for this). Shylock is what I might be. He is also what I know I can never be, because of my own awful pragmatism, because I do not trust the law so starkly as he does, since I know the terrors of art made tongue-tied by authority, and because I trade only in imaginary hearts—though I know no more than Shylock what these hearts are, no more than I know what it profits me to have them, or what losses that profit incurs. Searching for my listener's hearts, I ask the same question that Shylock asks his friend Tubal about Jessica and her Christian husband: "No news of them, why so? And I know not what's spent in the search. Why thou loss upon loss—the thief gone with so much, and so much to find the thief." Perhaps this is what my readers say by way of complaint, after centuries of trying to find out my mind and heart: "No news of them, why so? And I know not what's spent in the search." Shylock is my singularity, what cannot be named or measured or converted. So when will I be able to say, as my wizard of his mooncalf, "This thing of darkness I acknowledge mine"?

Chapter Three

SHYLOCK'S NOTHING

Farewell, thou art too dear for my possessing,
And like enough thou know'st thy estimate;
The charter of thy worth gives thee releasing,
My bonds in thee are all determinate.
For how do I hold thee but by thy granting,
And for that riches where is my deserving?
The cause of this fair gift in me is wanting,
And so my patent back again is swerving.
Thyself thou gav'st, thy own worth then not knowing,
Or me, to whom thou gav'st it, else mistaking,
So thy great gift, upon misprision growing,
Comes home again, on better judgment making.
    Thus have I had thee as a dream doth flatter:
    In sleep a king, but waking no such matter.

The force of this sonnet, number 87, lies in how the metaphor of the relinquished bond seeks to contain both grief over loss and anger at betrayal. Calling an end to a love affair, the poem offers a slowed-down, studious cost accounting, retrospectively imposing a vision of that affair's uncertain origins in worthlessness and misjudgment. It posits the undoing of a gift that evolved out of misprision, trying to correct a kind of misbirth in time past; it makes of a loss something that comes home again, as if all losses in time could be prevented or undone, though the poet knows they cannot be. In this oddly one-sided divorce, the pain of loss, which includes a suspicion of erotic betrayal, is veiled through a tone of disenchanted financial realism; the economic language also reinterprets darkly the origins of the love which that loss undoes, pointing to the errors which provoked that love. The legal terms of possession, bond, release, charter, and patent all carry a hovering sexual sense; the language is stroked as if it were the only means left to negotiate the breach, which is partly why it lends a hallucinatory bitterness to the whole movement. "Too dear" means both too precious and too costly, though the currency is not specified; the poem tries to measure what cannot be measured or told. We do not know exactly what "riches" are in question here, what it means to possess them or deserve them, or to have their ownership (paradoxically) "swerve back" to its origins. One thing that marks the mystery, the crisis in judgment, is that the metaphoric terms themselves shift subtly from the figure of a broken legal contract—an exchange of property or a loan of money—to the idea of an erring gift. And these figurative terms yield in the end to something different again, the idea of possession as a dream of royal mastery which vanishes at the moment of waking, becoming "no such matter." In the course of the sonnet, memory turns on its axis as much as love. The language of the poem inhabits an ambiguous middle ground. Is it praise or blame, a reflection of honorable business or of shoddy dealing?

For all that the poet seems to speak of loss of possession shadowed by the loss of self-worth—ironically defending against a deprivation he cannot really control—what strikes me in reading this text is the speaker's air of mastery. The ironic strength of self-possession is audible in the steady march of its falling, feminine rhymes—possessing, releasing, granting, deserving, wanting, swerving, knowing, mistaking, growing, making, flatter, matter.

The staged self-contempt in this mourning poem barely conceals a deeper contempt for the unnamed beloved, an object whose love is so untrustworthy and self-enclosed, whose "gifts" may be only the result of the speaker's power to make something out of nothing. (I am reminded here of the ambivalent praise, likewise masking a sense of contempt, for the aristocratic beloved object in sonnet 94, "They that have pow'r to hurt," one of those "sweetest things" who "turn sourest by their deeds.") Sonnet 87 in fact witnesses the poet-lover's recognition of his own powers. This is especially clear if we read the apparently rhetorical questions in lines 5 and 6 as real questions: "For how do I hold thee but by thy granting, / And for that riches where is my deserving?" We can take the next line as an answer to these questions: "The cause of this fair gift in me is wanting"—construing "wanting" in the sense of "desiring" as much as "lacking," so that the line speaks of the deserts and gift of the poet's desire itself, the constitutive power of a wanting that faces down a treacherous lack in his lover and in himself. He asks to hold on to what was perhaps never even properly given. Here the founding misprision of great gifts in question is not only that committed by the young man; the poem refers to a power of misprision in the poet, his power to convert drossy matter into gold, to make loss breed stranger riches. This is how he survives and masters loss. Line 7 thus reads as a recognition of the sources of what strength the poet after all does have or keep, that is, the strength of his need. It says not "I lack in myself that which would make you want to love me," but rather "The cause of this fair gift in me—my love for you and your love for me—is my desire itself, a desire grounded in lack, in what is wanting." We see here a relinquishment that grounds possession in very loss. Commandingly, the poem takes a stand on what the beloved cannot know of himself. It speaks to the poet's power to possess the world through his own generosity in embracing the misprisions of desire, opening himself up to the categorical errors of wanting, his own and that of others, mining his own withheld rage, contempt, and self-doubt for profits of the strangest sort. In this we can hear a basic note of Shakespearean imagination itself—its intricate investments in loss, its mining or banking of deprivation. The bond is kept in its very relinquishment. ("Strongly spent is synonymous with kept," says Robert Frost of how one measures the commitments of the poet's will as it braves alien entanglements.) The profits of the poem are grounded in an uncanny investment in the quality of nothing. The sonnet speaks for a strength gained through an embrace of the negative, what William Flesch describes as Shakespeare's "spectral generosity."

Shakespeare's sonnets seem to belong to the mid 1590s (though the dating is a murky matter), roughly contemporary with *The Merchant of Venice*, written around 1596. This may account for the play's peculiar crossing of concerns with the sonnets, its way of echoing their paradoxical, self-enfolding, and self-canceling pictures of desire, their jamming up together of the language of possession and dispossession, praise and slander. The sonnets are texts in which, as W. H. Auden says, the poet explores the shapes and limits of his own poetic powers. I have sometimes imagined what it would be like to hear the sad, self-wounding merchant Antonio recite sonnet 87 to Bassanio, for whom he hazarded so much, as the young man turns away to another, richer love, or to hear Shylock repeat these lines to Antonio after Shylock's own bond with the hated merchant is voided in court, and the cost of that bond becomes so nakedly clear. "Farewell, thou art too dear for my possessing." Could Shylock speak this line to his absent daughter Jessica, converted to Christianity and enriched with his gold, spending it so carelessly? In the play itself, Shylock, when he contemplates Jessica's departure, delivers himself of a more nightmarish sort of cost accounting:

Why there, there, there, there! A diamond gone cost me two thousand ducats in Frankfurt! The curse never fell upon our nation till now, I never felt it till now. Two thousand ducats in that, and other precious,

precious jewels! I would my daughter were dead at my foot, and the jewels in her ear: would she were hearsed at my foot, and the ducats in her coffin. . . . Why thou loss upon loss—the thief gone with so much, and so much to find the thief. (3.1.66–74)

At this moment Shylock gives himself over to a knowledge or wish he can scarcely understand. What kind of waking dream king is he here? We get a glimpse of another world, in Shylock's mind, also at his feet, in the empty place where he stands onstage, look-ing and pointing down at what isn't there. The eloquence of this is a prose eloquence—that seems crucial. It is not the eloquence of an enlarged consciousness, such as we feel in Hamlet, Lear, or Macbeth. It is an eloquence of deprivation. It is an eloquence of being, yet also an eloquence of nonexistence, and of curious depen-dence. Shakespeare means to show us the shape but also the agony of this eloquence, the agony of what it asks and cannot get, and the agony of what it costs that cannot be restored.

It is not at all clear what kind of work this eloquence seeks to accomplish. Are its motives, to borrow Kenneth Burke's catego-ries, those of map, prayer, or dream? The words are not quite a formal curse, or a prayer, since no higher powers are invoked. Nor do they align the desolate Shylock with the consolations of an es-tablished ritual of mourning. This is no Kaddish to be said over a child who has converted to Christianity, such as an Orthodox Jew might utter. Shylock declares, outrageously, that "the curse never fell upon our nation till now, I never felt it till now." I'm not sure if his use of the word "curse" echoes Old Testament sources, such as Lamentations—where God's curse on the sinful nation of Israel includes the loss of a temple and a kingdom, exile and enslavement, as well the curse of impotent rage and bitterness against Israel's enemies—or whether the word reflects, unconsciously, the lan-guage of Christian tradition, in which Jews were cursed both for their part in the death of Christ and for their continuing failure to recognize his godhead. In either case, Shylock declares, a larger history of Jewish suffering becomes truly palpable to him only in its being translated both by the loss of his gold and his daughter and by the pain of trying to undo that loss; these contingent, private afflictions for Shylock point more truly to the sources of the curse. It is an apprehension by which he cuts himself off from Jewish history as much as he aligns himself with it. (In this he is a little like Job, refusing the comforts of a conventional, moralistic explanation of human suffering.) For this loss Shylock proposes a compensation that compounds the loss itself. He wishes his daughter back, but only when she is dead. He wishes the jewels in the coffin with her, preserved together, as something to be buried, but perhaps also—we cannot exclude this thought—kept together like some ghoulish mummy-trophy in his house. You could see this image as Shylock's translation of Portia's caskets, those boxes which seek to divide out and emblematically contain or localize the gifts of death, folly, and beauty, also the unmeasurable gifts of hazard and chance, the gifts of time. The translation shows a fanatic immediacy impossible to imagine in Belmont. The lines focus on what in his daughter is unreadable, what cannot be measured. (Recall the astonishment of Lamentations at the fallen children of Zion: once "comparable to fyne golde, how are thei estemed as earthen pitchers, even the worke of the hands of the potter!" [4:2]). Shylock wants his jewels back, yet he imagines them transformed into ornaments for his dead daughter, and reduced to nothing but earrings. The fantasy is at once vengeful and recuperative, also sacrificial, since the gold and jewels will be buried away in the earth along with the ornamented corpse. Neither gold nor child is quite confused with the other; neither is tradable for the other; there is no easy logic of exchange here. The child is no longer a child; the jewels are more than jewels. Indeed, in this sacrificial bundling of the two we can sense an ironic sort of generosity, a grim mirror of, and a revenge against, the prodigality of Jessica that Tubal reports to Shylock in this scene. She is still, in Shylock's fantasy, decked as a bride. He is in the coffin with her, buried alive. It is at best a perverse and self-wounding generosity. It is the generosity of a god who is at once creator and destroyer, idol maker and iconoclast.

"I would my daughter were dead at my foot, and the jewels in her ear: would she were hearsed at my foot, and the ducats in her coffin." The hallucinatory force of this comes partly from Shylock's use of repetition, by which he at once marks and seeks to compensate for his loss, a device I will say more about below. The mysterious quality of the lines also lies in his ambiguous description of what he wishes to see, what he "would." He wishes to see his daughter and to put her away at the same moment, he wants both to have his jewels and to bury them. The description is ambiguous: To be hearsed is not necessarily to be dead. For jewels to be "in" an ear is not the same as for gold to be "in" a coffin, and Jessica's ears are "hers" differently from the way a coffin is "hers." Thus imagined, Jessica hovers in an uncertain state—both alive and dead, something between a mere corpse and the body of an individual, she is at once embalmed and galvanized. The gold in the casket is riches, trash, ornament, and a symbol of love all at the same time. It gains by proximity to the imagined body of Shylock's daughter its own unsettling life, both natural and unnatural. You might think here of Ophelia in her tomb, or Desdemona on her wedding bed, or of Pericles' Thaisa, supposed dead and thrown out to sea in a coffin filled with perfumes and jewels. What animation there is in Shylock's fantasy entails a nightmarish transformation of what's implied by the coming to life of the statue of a dead wife at the end of *The Winter's Tale*, since Shylock's words imply both a burial and an exhumation. How does this fantasy answer his loss? What does Shylock get back in it? One could say that he gets back his own heart, though it is hard to say what sort of heart. It is a heart of loss as much as a heart of stone. ("For where your treasure is, there wil your heart be also," says Christ in the sermon on the mount [Matthew 6:21]. The reverse of this can also be true.) Or is it that Shylock fantasizes getting back his generative power, lodged in both his child and in his ducats, his power to make gold breed?

Shylock's dream of getting Jessica back here provides a grim mockery of his own despair and sense of violation, in which he recognizes perhaps what it means that he controls the circulation of money in a world where he has no property, not even in his daughter, unless it is her corpse. What bank, treasury, or temple, in Venice or in Belmont, could hold such a casket? Shylock's imaginary coffin is a version of his inner life, a death and a life buried within him, somehow unburied here, set out visibly before him, before us—conjured up like a hallucination onstage. These lines are a vortex that sucks all distinct values into itself, like a kind of inverted cornucopia, a nothing that is pregnant with stranger plenty. Perhaps he is experimenting, as he will in the trial scene, with a version of exchange that will bring exchange to an end, cancel all his debts, an exchange that becomes a means of revenge, even as it entraps him further.

In trying to understand these lines, I find a useful point of reference in Anne Carson's *Economy of the Unlost*, a book that discusses the archaic Greek lyric poet Simonides, author of spare, ghostly, often ironic epitaphs and poems of praise, said also to be the inventor of the art of memory. Simonides was a poet who, she argues, discovered himself at the threshold between a gift economy and something like modern commodity exchange (hence his understanding of memory itself as "both commodity and gift, both wage and grace"). The first poet to insist on being paid directly for his words—rather than surviving through the more traditional means of aristocratic patronage—Simonides created an art that embraces its own poverty and parsimony, even its own miserliness, a poetry that sees profit in spaces of deprivation, in the poetic word's paradoxical, often fragile recompense for catastrophe. Such poetry, as Aristotle says of money in the *Nichomachean Ethics*, is "a guarantee of exchange in the future for something not given in the present." "Not given" may for the poet mean "taken away." In her book, Carson places Simonides against Paul Celan, a poet haunted by the vaster wastes of the death camps, whose embrace of the negative and the poor is a ground of more baffling returns and

impossible compensations, words stripped down to gifts of knowing loss, parings away and compressions of sense, "diving words"
that took up the German language as a contaminated inheritance.
In the company of these two writers, Simondes and Celan, Carson
develops a vision of the poet as one who finds himself "provoked
by a perception of absence within what others regard as a full and
satisfactory present. . . . He does not seek to refute or replace that
[supposedly full] world but merely to indicate its lacunae, by posi-
tioning alongside the world of things we see an uncanny prostasis
of things invisible, although no less real. Without poetry these two
worlds would remain unconscious of one another." Seeking a bridge
between the ancient and the modern writer, Carson on a number
of occasions points to the eerie, delicate, and harrowing power that
Shakespeare in *King Lear* lends to the play's proliferating "nothings," its multiple "nevers," and its never-completed laying bare of
things "worse." She might also have adduced, more ironically, the
words of Shakespeare's Jewish moneylender in a passage like the
one I have quoted, where he makes of Jessica's absence the ground
of a frightening vision of compensation or profit, tries to defeat her
absence with a double supply that opens up an unseen world, an
uncannier past and future. Shylock, we should recall, addresses his
loss itself as "thou"—"thou loss upon loss"—as he would his own
lost daughter, if not, idolatrously, his own lost gold, marking the
need with which he conjures from nothing a more terrible nothing.

What do they know of nothing, these souls who pay for my words in the
mouths of the players? They forget them the instant they hear them. Do they
know what they pay for? What's purchased in these words? I scarcely know
myself what it is, my words change their face so madly in being paid for, they
turn into things I do not know, more and less than I meant, mine own and
not mine own. Not like Ovid's water boy, Narcissus, whose plenty made him
poor, I make an abundance of this nothing, this not knowing, this loss of my
words, this famine of speech. These nothings breed like ewes and goats, like
gold and silver. What do the listeners take into their ears? Foreign or false

coinage? forbidden meat? a ghost? a shred? poison? a toy? a pretty picture? How do my words lodge in their hearts, those caskets I cannot open? And will they open the right casket when they need to? It is hard to know what to hazard for opening the heart. Have I lost their hearts? I cannot tell. Their hearts are drowned deep. Would they were lying at my foot with my words in their ears. Would they were hearsed at my foot with their hearts in my hand. A miserable folly it seems, this need to put forth such words, empty as they are, yet out of that folly one begins to write, called to it by those who come to listen. This foolishness is buried within me as in a coffin, I can open it to them if not to myself.

Chapter Four

THE HOUSE OF THE
THREE CASKETS

Portia's house is the site of the other crucial caskets of the play, the three coffers or coffins of lead, silver, and gold among which her prospective husbands must choose. The quality of Shylock's presence in this play depends on Belmont's being a place that excludes him, a place where he is indeed scarcely mentioned, and then never by name (he is, in Belmont, only "the Jew," or the "enemy"). There are lines that run between Belmont and Venice and the plots that unfold in each, though how much the two worlds mirror or oppose one another, what the gravitational pull is between them, are questions one never exhausts. Shylock's money funds Bassanio's voyage to Belmont in quest for his bride, and it is from Belmont in turn that Portia journeys to Venice to save Antonio. If Belmont is her home it is also, one might say, her law school, the place where she learns things about the workings of contracts, desire, authority, paternal will, self-blinding need, and even revenge that will give her the edge at the trial in Venice. And if Belmont presents itself as a purer, more ideal world of romance, less bound to the hazards of business, more courtly, generous—a villa designed by Palladio with frescoes by Veronese—it speaks also of gold and fortune, and of the fears and restraints that affect the life of things in business-driven Venice. As William Empson says of double plots more generally, the two worlds are positioned so as to suggest the maximum amount of magic in their connection combined with the maximum possibility for critical judgment.

The world of Belmont often makes me think of F. Scott Fitzgerald. I can imagine the novelist studying the text of *The Merchant of Venice* for certain atmospheric effects, images of a sky "thick inlaid with patens of bright gold," or certain plays of silence and distance, ironies of perspective, a sense of glowing surfaces set over uncertain depths. Especially as glimpsed in act 5, we sense the deep ceremonious charm, generosity, and play, even the innocence made possible by the magic of money; we sense as well how the place is haunted by a vague awareness of the sacrifices or shames that subtend this innocence, and the guards in place against knowing these more clearly. One senses that the rich imagine themselves and others wrongly, and are wrongly imagined by others. Listening to the banter of Lorenzo and Jessica about wronged, endangered, or treacherous lovers—Cressida, Thisbe, Dido, and Medea—you need something of Fitzgerald's radar for the pathos of such bonds, the eventual wasting or sickening of love defended thus from reality and from knowing its own ambivalence; one senses a love disowned by its need for a golden sustenance, or by being turned into a coin, a neat form of exchange. The scene suggests gold's mysterious gravitational pull, its way of working at both surface and depth. Fitzgerald's lovers, being caught within the orbit of money or by wishes deformed by the presence of money, tend to enter into the wrong relation to both their past and their future, and to their dependence on one another. Could one see Belmont in the light of Gatsby's seashore house, with its elaborate displays of wealth, shifting flood of visitors, and hidden stays of longing? I am thinking even more of *Tender Is the Night*, with its picture of the self-betraying charm and charity of Dick Diver, his inability to divide care for his beautiful, increasingly lunatic wife from dependence on her fortune, the growing vanity of his professional ambitions as a doctor of souls, the slow wearing away of his love, and his eventual exile. Fitzgerald is Shakespearean in seeing below his mansions and hotels (or exclusive sanatoriums), with their endless flow of inventive luxury, the sense of lives gone inevitably wrong, gone wrong even through the means by which his characters seek to make them right. As in Shakespeare, the romance is not trivial; the sense of youthful charm and the passion may be real enough, human and true enough. Yet the charm is also evanescent, unable to face something, caught in a subtly false paradise or trusted too far; it creates an aesthetic space in which things concealed are exposed against one's will, where a subtle shame or embarrassment creeps in. So we see Fitzgerald writing of Diver, in Shakespearean cadences, that he was "paying some tribute to things unforgotten, unshriven, unexpurgated," this man who knows, as he says, that "the strongest guard is placed at the gateway to nothing . . . maybe because the condition of emptiness is too shameful to be divulged." Fitzgerald would have relished G. Wilson Knight's observations about how, in *The Merchant of Venice*, gold as a soul symbol gets infected by gold as a synecdoche for commerce, both an exploitation of and a subjection to the world of hazard. The quest for gold shows as an attempt to control mutability, fear of death and loss, as well as madness. This fear of death and time is like a menacing bass note floating below the tenor aria of Lorenzo's ode to music, marring a central Renaissance symbol of the transformative power of human art, the guarantor of the soul's link to a distant, transcendent domain of harmony.

Shakespeare's Belmont has something about it at once dangerous and vaguely tacky. It's as if it housed brilliant children who toy with a nuclear reactor, or who forget that their imaginary palace is built of rags, bits of wood and paint, and plaster, everything found by accident, by chance, put together like a stage set. There is an archaic feel to the place, as readers have seen, and the sense of a fairy-tale order in the casket game. The brusk, knowing exchange of jests between Portia and Nerissa about the various suitors introduces us to this world, its waywardness, conventionality, and pretence, yet the arcane ritual choice orders their world in a fashion they cannot so lightly put away. At the center of this world is a feeling of menace and a ferocious will to contain that menace. This feeling comes through in the way Portia and Nerissa appeal so readily to national stereotypes—the drunken German, the peacock Frenchman, the ignorant Englishman, his manners a patchwork of others'—in order to keep at bay something not so trivial, the fear of those unwanted marriage suits, and the knowledge of how much Portia is made subject to those suits by the terms of her father's will, a will that yet seeks to defend her against false suitors. The need to contain unknown possibilities is part of what strikes one in the way that meaning is deployed in the symbolic framing of the caskets themselves. In the sequence of discoveries—the death's head within the gold casket, the fool's head within the silver, the portrait of beautiful Portia within the lead—one feels an attempt to divide up the ambivalent domain of human experience into three distinct symbols, three distinct lessons about the shape of human life and desire, the site of such wounds as draw around them the most powerful cathexes. One might recall, by contrast, the more interwoven, more frankly ambivalent associations of the scene in *Hamlet* where we see the skull of a dead clown unearthed from the place where the corpse of drowned, flower-strewn Ophelia will be buried. The play structures the casket game so that it frames a dramatic contrast between inner and outer, surface sign and hidden truth, illusion and disillusionment, as each suitor pulls out the concealed symbol from within the closed box. Each of the three suitors offers a beautiful rhetorical set piece—Morocco reading gold as a symbol of heroic desire, Arragon reading silver as a symbol of noble desert, Bassanio taking lead as an emblem of plainness, of humility undisguised by the gilding of lies. The sequence works by a kind of reverse alchemy, from gold back to lead, or, perhaps, the discovery of true gold, Portia's love, within lead. The progress is compelling;

it has a fairy-tale inevitability. Still, one feels just how ad hoc each interpretation of both the caskets and their emblematic contents is, and how much is left unspoken about the other associations that circulate around them. Bassanio's speech about the virtues of plainness turns out to be right, as it were; yet in what follows, his words move so swiftly from praise of plainness to praise of the fantastic meshes and mysteries of human beauty that one is struck by their opportunism. This is not to dismiss any of the speeches as false, but only to suggest how many threads the scene throws out into other realms of meaning, how much the rigid structure of understanding and intention provided by the casket test feels itself like an attempt to contain, exclude, and make discrete what is otherwise so confusing.

The play of possibilities is nevertheless heightened by such constraint. Hence the feeling of a tormenting but inescapable, even beautiful, game. It is a vision of art. Imagine a dance choreographed by George Balanchine entitled "Three Caskets," a pendant to his "Four Temperaments" or, better, his "Jewels," which has a dance apiece for diamonds, rubies, and emeralds. Or imagine a shadow box created by Joseph Cornell, holding within its chambers emblems of order, menace, transience, longing, and isolation; wire meshes, hidden mirrors, broken glasses, star charts, compasses, coins, a doll's head, secret missives, and a plastic heart; a shelf of small glass bottles containing ashes, shells, crumpled paper, gold dust, and a dime-store ring; or silhouettes of lost ballerina daughters and unachievable soprano wives.

Sigmund Freud, in his 1913 essay "The Theme of the Three Caskets," registers the dreamlike ambivalence of the scene in Belmont, bringing to bear on his analysis all that he understands of dreams in his larger book, *The Interpretation of Dreams*. He points to the presence of energies whose repression is signaled by the overelaborateness of the ritual itself and the conspicuous irrelevance of so much of what Portia's suitors say about their choices. Within the romantic story about a lover who successfully finds his true love concealed in a chest of lead rather than in one of gold or silver, Freud sees another story. It is a story about a man's choice among three women, three objects of love, such as is represented in *King Lear* or the Judgment of Paris, even Cinderella. And hidden within this story, by reversal, is yet another, a fable in which the goddess of love reveals herself as the goddess of death; the pale, silent, leaden third, like Cordelia, points to death; it is a figure of mortality, warning us that we are all "part of nature and therefore subject to the immutable law of death." The scene of choice thus points to a story about the election of death over love, or about death itself as an object of desire, *thanatos* mingled with *eros*. One glimpses here, Freud argues, an ancient dream of man's being able to choose his own death or form of fate, instead of being overtaken by a death or fate that is beyond his control. In this fantasy, the menace at the heart of human experience becomes a gift, a form of blessing instead of a curse or the sign of an originary fall. The tragic image of Lear bearing his dead daughter in his arms turns into the redemptive picture of the old man being borne into eternity in the arms of a loving mother. The more bitter version of the scene, which Freud doesn't evoke, is glimpsed in Shylock's vengeful dream of his daughter's entombment, mastering her freedom of choice. Could we see Shylock as Lear bearing his dead daughter in his arms? Or can we imagine a dream in which Shylock sees Jessica, in turn, bearing him into eternity?

As Marjorie Garber points out, Freud's essay curiously evades or occludes certain crucial aspects of Shakespeare's story. Shylock, the Jewish father, is not mentioned at all, but even more striking is that the essay pays no attention to Portia, the overseer and prize of the casket tests, or to how her agency, desire, and anxiety figure in the scene. That lack is partly supplied by Freud's student, Theodor Reik, in his book of literary and autobiographical reflections, *The Secret Self*. Reik evokes in Portia a fairy-tale princess such as Carlo Gozzi's Turandot, who tests her princely suitors with three riddles and cuts off their heads when they cannot answer. She is also the sphinx in the Oedipus legend, who guards the gate of Thebes and tears to pieces those who cannot answer her question about the creature who walks on four legs in the morning, two at noon, and three in the evening. Such analogies suggest that Portia is not only the golden fleece sought by Jason—Bassanio's analogy—but also the never-sleeping dragon who guards that fleece. She is, furthermore, a version of the enchantress Medea, whose magic gives Jason the very means to put that dragon to sleep. Portia does make a riddle of herself; the menace of death or castration first emerges only at a distance, say, in the oath that all suitors must swear, that if they fail the casket test they must both keep silent about their choices and never woo women in marriage again. The association of Portia with a riddling enchantress comes out more strongly at the trial, in her way of managing the death and life of Antonio and Shylock, and her showing of what tricksy, vengeful logic subtends her call for mercy.

I have never been convinced that Bassanio finds out the right casket by listening to the song Portia calls for, where the lines all rhyme with "lead": "Tell me where is fancy bred, / Or in the heart, or in the head? / How begot, how nourishèd?" (3.2.63–65). The questions are real enough, whatever we think, as are those raised in Bassanio's speech before he chooses the casket, where he reflects on the uneasy relation of surfaces and depths, glister and gold, pride and humility. If his speech feels uneasy, it is because he seems to be acting in a dream, or trying by language to keep alive the complex dream of Belmont even before he wins it—a dream that combines a sense of penetration and possession, bondage and freedom, secrecy and exposure, spirit gold and physical gold. Here in particular we start to see how the idea of Belmont underlies Venice, feeds its ambition to find in gold a perfect vehicle for or solvent of desire; we see also how Venice, symbol of raw, mercantile commerce, underlies the romance of Belmont, its air of heroic fortune being bound to fortune in the form of money.

Having made his choice, Bassanio asks for its truth to be ratified by Portia's own spoken words, and not just by the scroll that accompanies her picture. His promised wife replies with words that attempt, in a more local way, to make the contingencies of human choice take on the look of something more magical, fatal, even as she speaks with a sense of palpable relief at being released from the double bind of her father's casket game. She unlocks herself from her own coffer. The speech combines a sense of exposure with a sense of self-possession, negotiating an exchange that is also a transformation of selfhood; she at once acknowledges Bassanio's acquisitive instincts in wooing her and repossesses them for herself:

> You see me, Lord Bassanio, where I stand,
> Such as I am. Though for myself alone
> I would not be ambitious in my wish
> To wish myself much better, yet for you
> I would be trebled twenty times myself,
> A thousand times more fair, ten thousand times
> More rich, that only to stand high in your account
> I might in virtues, beauties, livings, friends,
> Exceed account. But the full sum of me
> Is sum of something: which to term in gross
> Is an unlessoned girl, unschooled, unpractised.   (3.2.149–59)

Turning from possession to education, she declares her happiness in being young enough to learn, and finding herself in a position to be taught by one such as Bassanio, "her lord, her governor, her king." The speech then turns from teaching back to matters of ownership and mastery:

> Myself, and what is mine, to you and yours
> Is now converted. But now I was the lord

Of this fair mansion, master of my servants,
Queen o'er myself; and even now, but now,
This house, these servants, and this same myself
Are yours, my lord's. I give them with this ring,
Which when you part from, lose, or give away,
Let it presage the ruin of your love,
And be my vantage to exclaim on you.   (3.2.166–74)

Portia here tries to master a felt metamorphosis, to control the loss or giving over of herself as a marriage portion. She makes a gift of both her imaginary insufficiency and her wished-for hyper-sufficiency, makes a gift not of what she is but of what she might be. This speech, one feels, is so carefully controlled. She no sooner makes that ring the vehicle of her gift to Bassanio than she disowns him of it by cataloging the consequences of that gift's vanishing, binding him (as she is bound?) to fears of loss, dispossession, and shame. It's a little like Othello's cruelly warning Desdemona of the costs of losing her handkerchief just when he knows, he thinks, that she has already lost it. The power of the lines comes from the simultaneous awareness of their remarkable candor—one's sense that Portia here reveals her love, vulnerability, and fear of losing control—and their cunning mastery, by which she holds on to things even as she transfers them to Bassanio. Especially in her handing him her ring—a gesture by which she seems to officiate at her own marriage—Portia at one moment gives herself away and keeps herself. She makes herself a more incalculable object; she acknowledges her own desire and need, her wish to be more than what she is, yet she makes that desire, that need, an aspect of her person. Here if anywhere she makes herself both a riddle and the riddle's solution. Marc Shell sees in Portia's speech a commitment to the mysterious logic of exchange, here localized in the domestic and erotic sphere, that mirrors Shylock's commitment to his bond. This reading, about which I will say more below, works only if we keep our ears open to Portia's extremity as well as to her mystifications of motive. The wish haunting both love and money here is audible in Portia's repeated appeal to something "more." This points not to the human wish for a concrete something, but to a principle of multiplication that challenges the idea of limits or accounting; it evokes the possibility of linking a worldly economy to something transcendental, even as it reflects the flatter, horizontal increments or "mores" of the money world—a connection shown more bluntly in Shylock's comparison of his moneymaking to the miracle of Laban's sheep.

Shakespeare indeed makes Portia evoke something of Shylock here, though she as yet knows nothing about him. If we are listening carefully, we catch her speech echoing words and cadences we have heard from Shylock himself in the scene that just precedes her climactic confrontation with Bassanio and its transformation of her status. That prior scene offers its own sort of climax, Shylock framing what it means to be a Jew, measuring in the face of humiliation and loss what remains of his person, and what sort of transformation he is now likely to undergo in the face of his daughter's betrayal. Both speeches open us up toward unprecedented, limitless worlds, even as they try to master them. Shylock's speech is so well known that it's a little hard to hear it, and we can restore the shock of it just by making clear its unspoken dialogue with Portia's words. In what follows, I have juxtaposed fragments of the speeches by both characters. It is less a dialogue than a duet or two-part invention, a piece of ensemble singing in which Shylock's words provide the dark undersong to the poised, golden notes of Portia's speech:

> You see me, Lord Bassanio, where I stand,
> Such as I am.

> *I am a Jew.*

>   Though for myself alone

38

I would not be ambitious in my wish
To wish myself much better,

Hath not a Jew eyes?

                    yet for you
I would be trebled twenty times myself,
A thousand times more fair, ten thousand times
More rich,

Two thousand ducats in that, and other precious, precious jewels. . . . Why
thou loss upon loss.

              that only to stand high in your account
I might in virtues, beauties, livings, friends,
Exceed account.

He hath . . . laughed at my losses, mocked at my gains, scorned my nation,
thwarted my bargains, cooled my friends, heated my enemies.

                  But the full sum of me

Hath not a Jew hands, organs, dimensions, senses, affections, passions?

Is sum of something:

Fed with the same food, hurt with the same weapons, subject to the same
diseases, healed by the same means?

               which to term in gross
Is an unlessoned girl, unschooled, unpractised;
Happy in this, she is not yet so old
But she may learn; happier than this,
She is not bred so dull but she can learn;

Happiest of all, is that her gentle spirit
Commits itself to yours to be directed
As from her lord, her governor, her king.

That villainy you teach me I will execute, and it shall go hard but I will better the instruction.

Myself, and what is mine, to you and yours
Is now converted.

If you wrong us, shall we not revenge? If we are like you in the rest, we will resemble you in that.

But now I was the lord
Of this fair mansion, master of my servants,
Queen o'er myself; and even now, but now,

The curse never fell upon our nation till now, I never felt it till now.

This house, these servants, and this same myself
Are yours, my lord's.

I would my daughter were dead at my foot, and the jewels in her ear.

I give them with this ring,

Out upon her! . . . It was my turquoise, I had it of Leah when I was a bachelor. I would not have given it for a wilderness of monkeys.

Which when you part from, lose, or give away,

Why thou loss upon loss—the thief gone with so much, and so much to find the thief.

Let it presage the ruin of your love,
And be my vantage to exclaim on you.

I'll plague him, I'll torture him. I am glad of it.

The effect of this is more startling if you read the lines out loud, as I have done with students, sometimes with the two speakers face to face, acknowledging each other, on other occasions placing them at a distance or simply back to back, as if neither were aware of the other's presence. The echoes can only be intentional. Shakespeare's ear is cunning this way. Part of the interest in this game is that Portia and Shylock speak from such opposing worlds of experience. Shylock would scorn the delicate erotic economies of Portia; Portia could not bear the violence of Shylock's words. She speaks as much to what repels us in Shylock as to what might make us suspicious of Portia, in particular, Shylock's thought of his own vengeful humanity and the grim fantasy of repossessing in one coffin his lost daughter and lost jewels. Portia, again, speaks for the sudden access of a new world, a world in ways poorer and harder to control, even as she feels herself flooded with the truth of a generosity that is keyed to a freedom of wish she had never known before, bound as her choices have been by the rules of the casket game. She suddenly feels this ritual and its hazard of lovers as a gift rather than an awful trap. The game suddenly opens toward a fantastic kind of cost accounting, even as she is conscious of employing a debased language of quantity. The generosity of that speech, as I once heard a young actor say, includes the playwright's generosity in providing the actor playing Portia with such lines to be spoken. They demand of the actor a matching generosity in giving herself over to the words, finding in them a vehicle for that risky sense of exposure and relinquishment of will that is crucial to the actor's work, since these are the means of opening up what funds of hidden wealth the actor carries inside. Despite this air of generosity, I can never banish a nervous sense of calculation, a holding on to what is given that suggests Portia's own anxiety about hazarding all she has in giving herself to her lover. She holds the reins still, and will tighten them further as the story unfolds. The parallel between Othello's speech and Portia's closing words about the ring is sharp: "I give them with this ring, / Which when you part from, lose, or give away, / Let it presage the ruin of your love." "Make it a darling like your precious eye. / To lose't or give't away were such perdition / As nothing else could match" (*Othello* 3.4.66–68). Kenneth Burke wrote that in Othello's words, which project the idea of private property into dimensions where it has no certain guarantees, we hear a note of dispossession, estrangement, and isolation, a promise of his own ruin. Something of this also hovers as a suggestion in Portia's words, especially as we hear them echoing Shylock's utterances. The sense of loss, the need to withhold what cannot be withheld, is more directly yet more strangely present in Shylock's words about Leah's ring, or the ring that he imagines to be Leah's. In describing the exchange he says he would never make, he measures the ring's worth against something that he knows to be, in a bitterly ironic combination, at once vast and empty: "I would not have given it for a wilderness of monkeys." (That wilderness is partly a vision of the city of Venice.)

The Shakespearean touch is in how these opposites haunt each other or show a troubling family resemblance, how each might come to seem the unconscious of the other, even though (or especially because?) Portia and Shylock never meet until act 4, and then only when each is curiously disguised. Reading Shakespeare teaches us to listen for just these sorts of doublings over of speech; we learn to mind them. Something of this constitutes the poet's discovery in the language of his drama of what we might call the exteriorized interior life. Ultimately, even this precarious balance is broken, as Shylock breaks out into darker solos, unmatched talk.

EXCHANGES

Shylock's wish to have his daughter back encoffined and bejeweled lays no explicit curse on that world of commerce of which he is both a useful cog and contemptible victim, nor does it directly address the workings of a Christian society that justifies his daughter's theft. It tries, in fact, to close off for a moment any larger world of relation. The fierce idiosyncrasy of his vision will reemerge at the trial, as Shylock hugs to himself a bond that has lost all apparent reference to anything we might call monetary profit, to any system of relation in the world itself other that which obtains between him and Antonio, or perhaps between him and his own words.

One can contrast to Shylock's vision the rages of Shakespeare's Timon after he finds that the world will not requite his generosity—indeed, that it seems to hold his generosity in contempt when his riches are exhausted. Timon had tried to make himself a god within a system of malicious and contaminated exchange, a pure creature of gift. There is a self-destructive blindness in his giving of gifts, as his loyal steward Flavius notes; it has no stop, it refuses all gifts in return, and so tempts empty flattery and praise. Timon indeed seems in flight, for reasons we do not know, from his own indebtedness, a debt whose origins are hard to find, seeming at once absolute and arbitrary. Perhaps that is why there is something disquieting about the way that riches in *Timon of Athens* are supplied, lost, and restored. Timon's friends are astonished when they find he is suddenly without means to pay his creditors; it may seem to us in retrospect as if all his generosity had been borrowed. Coldly refused help by all, Timon flees the city and isolates himself as a railing hermit. Digging for roots, the earth's minimal nourishment, the food of one who imagines himself eaten by the world, he discovers a mysterious cache of gold that draws the world to him again. This he throws back at those who come to him as a curse, a source of destructive power, even as his language lends it (and him) a certain vicious magnetism. Timon speaks the following lines to a group of thieves who come seeking coins; he frames a vision of nature as wholly taken over by theft, a world in which all exchange is privative and illegitimate:

> The sun's a thief, and with his great attraction
> Robs the vast sea; the moon's an arrant thief,
> And her pale fire she snatches from the sun;
> The sea's a thief, whose liquid surge resolves
> The moon into salt tears; the earth's a thief,
> That feeds and breeds by a composture stol'n
> From gen'ral excrement; each thing's a thief. (4.3.436–42)

For Timon, all creative work is reduced to theft. Gold itself he addresses as a "visible god" that makes "close impossibilities" possible, an infectious idol that destroys all social bonds and, as Philip Brockbank says, "puts to moral death the words 'love and judgement', 'disgraced', 'conscience', 'fool', 'courage', and, of course, 'good,'" or allows such words only a phantom life. Timon points to a kind of negative alchemy by which gold degrades the elements of nature into base matter rather than transmuting matter into gold.

Shylock, like Timon, assumes a cursing eloquence of his own in the course of the play. Yet as a play about gold, *The Merchant of Venice* mutes any such universalizing attack on a world of profit and loss as we find in *Timon of Athens*. The ironic contaminations of love or beauty by desire for gold are brought into view, as is the possible hypocrisy of moralizing over those contaminations (as in Bassanio's speech in choosing the leaden casket, where gold becomes a synecdoche for the corrupting powers of beautiful appearances). Yet it is hard to extract from the play so absolute a critique of the world that makes use of gold to organize its work and wants. There is nothing like Timon's broad satire of human want, nor anything like the hellish vision of gold being forged and hoarded in the Cave of Mammon, depicted in book 2 of Edmund Spenser's *Faerie Queene*, a place where desire for gold becomes an emblem of all human temptation by glory, knowledge, and power. Still less does the play support the more orthodox attack on usury offered in a work like Thomas Wilson's 1572 *Discourse upon Usury*, published a year after Parliament allowed by law a rate of 10 percent interest on all loans. Writing at a time of ever-expanding capitalist enterprise, when the use of tools of credit was increasingly severed from worries about supernatural sanction, Wilson—no detached cleric but a scholar of rhetoric and logic, a common lawyer, parliamentarian, and diplomat—envisions usurious practices as a kind of infection, parasitism, or devouring sickness that can spread itself through a whole nation and body politic. He sees the demand for interest—something that can slyly disguise itself as fair exchange—becoming a demonic principle with a life of its own, uncontainable, something that in time corrodes all natural bonds, contaminates even charitable loans of the old sort, and exposes all social relation to a proliferation of lack. Such an attack responds to a world in which, as Benjamin Nelson observes in his study *The Idea of Usury*, all "brothers" have become potential "others" and may thus be loaned money for profit without violating either Deuteronomy 23:19–20, which allows the Israelites to practice usury only with strangers or aliens, or the Christian ideal of universal brotherhood. Antonio's bitter words to Shylock, "Lend it rather to thine enemy," echo patristic ideas of usury as a means of aggression and revenge, an extension of the violence of war, but they represent an isolated moment of rage. And overall, Shylock's vision of his profit as mirroring Jacob's miraculous multiplication of sheep holds a fascination that is never confuted by, say, the Aristotelian or Aquinian argument that usury is a species of unnatural begetting, the selling and buying of nothing, something implicit in Antonio's disdaining of interest as "a breed for barren metal." The muting of such attacks comes partly from the fact that, as W. H. Auden writes, the play conveys a sense of money not as mere profit or means of purchase, but as a symbol of man's dependence on the world, the medium through which, paradoxically, we may accept others as brothers, even if it can also be abused. ("Credit," we should remember, means "he believes, he has faith in.") Money ideally should be a means of social glue, a vehicle, for some, of love. Nor does the play directly attack the basis of banking or moneylending more generally, the idea that not just gold and goods but debt or indebtedness themselves may be bought and sold, calculated, summed, saved, and exchanged—that even time itself, as Wilson suggests, can become a commodity to be bought and sold.

The dangers of the business world take on subtler, more elusive forms in this play. Trying to explain Antonio's mysterious sadness, Solanio suggests that it must be anxiety over his mercantile ventures; he evokes an image of the world as itself wholly threatening to such ventures. Antonio's mind, he says, is "tossing on the ocean" along with his boats. We are in a world where "fortune" as a name for commerce starts to replace or seeks to control the medieval idea of fortune as "luck" or "chance," a cosmic principle of fallenness, even as commerce must face its own endless subjection to chance and contingency:

> Believe me, sir, had I such venture forth,
> The better part of my affections would
> Be with my hopes abroad. I should be still

Plucking the grass to know where sits the wind,
Piring in maps for ports, and piers, and roads;
And every object that might make me fear
Misfortune to my ventures, out of doubt
Would make me sad.   (1.1.15–22)

Solanio's companion Salarino enlarges on this, suggesting that if he
were Antonio, merely blowing on his soup would make him think
of dangerous winds, that the sand of hourglasses would speak of
shallow shoals, and that the very walls of the church where he
might seek comfort would remind him only of the rocks, "Which
touching but my gentle vessel's side / Would scatter all her spices
on the stream, / Enrobe the roaring waters with my silks" (32–
35), making the profits of the voyage into nothing, or at best the
momentary, mocking ornaments of the treacherous natural world.
Antonio denies that any such fears explain his sadness. Yet this
early and curiously eroticized conjuring up of the world of hazard
and its violence haunts subsequent scenes, scenes where hazard
takes on more local incarnations, not only as part of nature but
as part of the human world. It is not perhaps surprising that, in
this play, the dangers of sea and shore invade the spaces of the
city, both public and private (even the emblem of time itself, the
hourglass). Shakespeare is imagining the ways in which one always
feels the presence of the sea and its weather in the streets of Venice.
Hearing Solanio and Salarino's conjurings of watery disaster, I always think of an image in Geffrey Whitney's *Choice of Emblemes*
(1586), something copied from an original in the emblem book of
Andrea Alciati, who himself adapted it from a poem in the Greek
Anthology in which an allegorical statue of *Kairos*—timeliness,
opportunity, occasion—describes and explains itself. In Whitney,
we see an emblem of "Occasion" as a tall, classical nude, her heels
winged in a reminder of Mercury ("To showe, how lighte I flie
with little winde"), standing with her right foot slightly raised and
her left planted at the center of a moving wheel that rides on the

unquiet surface of the sea. In her extended right hand she holds an open razor, and in her left a long trailing scarf that floats around her shoulders and back. The most significant detail, however, is her hair, with a long forelock blown in front of her, waiting to be seized, but cut short behind, giving no purchase to those who come too late. In the background of the scene float a few ships with puffed sails; the perspective in the woodcut is crude enough to make either the ships seem like miniature boats or the woman herself like a giant. The emblem is an image of the intimate world of chance and change that haunts Shakespeare's play. Occasion here is an incarnation of the goddess Fortune, one of the few pagan deities to survive from Roman times into the Middle Ages, a goddess whose ambiguous powers (and whose ambiguity *as* a power, an agent rather than a name for mere accident) are invoked throughout *The Merchant of Venice*. We should recall here that Shylock himself bears a razor, and calculates the dangers of the sea.

In this play, business is something as general and equivocal in its powers as what Shakespeare calls "nature." There are no purely economic bonds at work here, any more than there are purely erotic bonds. Such bonds are always tangled up with something else, and their very liability to be so tangled is what gets explored so subtly. Solanio's word "affections," referring in the above-quoted lines to some quantifiable piece of mental investment, will in later scenes refer variously to rational wishes, desires, passions, and almost animal motions of instinct. I think here of Harold Goddard's account of Antonio's melancholy and ultimately suicidal self-pity. This sadness takes its origin, he argues, neither in mere fears about his money nor in repressed homosexual love for Bassanio, but rather in a confusion of his mercantile and erotic desires so relentless, and so unacknowledged, that each domain of desire can only sicken the other. If Antonio becomes, in Angus Fletcher's words, "a psychopath of the business world," it is not because he's a merchant, or even because he can't quite separate commerce from usury, but rather because he wants his money to do what it cannot. It is the melancholy of his relation to this world that counts, his sad way of standing within the realm of time, chance, luck, and hazard. He wants to stand apart from what he wants also to make use of; he wants to make of his isolation the one stable, absolute form of fate outside the world of time. Antonio seems to want to make time indifferent, not so much to make it stand still as to make it flexible, generous. For him, there is always more money to be had, always more love to be given away. In this his isolation takes on a life of its own; his defense becomes a symptom, a mask that possesses him, fixates him. With a kind of pathological generosity, he isolates himself from a merchant's ordinary fears, refusing to acknowledge the reality of the chances, gifts, and exchanges of which the world of international commerce is only the most extravagant emblem. Shylock—who is, ironically, the only one who will loan him money—comes to stand in the place of everything he would push away. He stands in for the sea of hazard, its profits and its depredations. He is the worldly breeding ground of chances for profit; his gold and silver breed mysteriously like the spotted sheep in the Jacob and Laban story, whereas Antonio sees himself as the "tainted wether of the flock." Antonio's is the will to sacrifice as much as the will to isolation, the will to become the one thing sacred enough, cursed or blessed enough, to be removed from the world. This, if anything, accounts for his hatred of Shylock, who seems able to adapt himself to that world with a certain chameleon-like quickness. Shylock is both the thing Antonio hates and the creature who in his activities is closest to him, his unacknowledged double, as Goddard sees (in parallel to René Girard's stark commentary on the play). The Jew is a figure who in his appetites calls the bluff of Antonio's wonted purity, reminds him of what his compulsive isolation defends him against.

Somehow Shakespeare has intuited what it means that usury was forced onto the Jews of medieval Europe as a way of isolating them, making them more hated, insofar as it forced onto them that aspect of the economy which was most unsettlingly suspect and paradoxically powerful, a thing that whole states were dependent on. He knows that the questions of Shylock's being a Jew and of his being a moneylender cannot be pried apart.

Harold Fisch sees *The Merchant of Venice* as haunted by questions spurred by the idea of covenant, the possibility of a human choice in which one is actively engaged or made responsible to a higher power; it implies a relation between persons or worlds that combines the contractual with the compulsive. The idea of covenant has its origins in Hebraic notions of a sacral contract and is brought powerfully into play by impulses within Reformation theology, with its focus on the relation of the individual soul to a saving divinity, cut off from any mediations provided by the sacramental machinery of the church. Furthermore, as Fisch points out, the idea of covenant readily takes on more secular forms at this moment in history. It is useful to those engaged in a world of commerce, since it points to a species of pact that is mobile, shifting, and contingent, caught up in time rather than bound by a fixed eternal order. The appeal is more to inward conscience than to outward law. During a moment when commerce is expanding its scope and seeking ideological justifications for its work, the idea of covenant allows strange intersections of the sacred with the economic and erotic. "Man is invited to participate with the 'metaphysical powers' to embark on a joint enterprise, but he cannot tell for what it is they invite him."

We need not wonder why so often in the post-Reformation world the covenant or contract is represented in the diabolical form as a pact with the powers of darkness. The men of the new age sensed the threat to the traditional orderly inherited world of medieval Christendom which the covenant theology posed, with its more dynamic, challenging, and earthbound ethical character, and consequently the imagination prompted them to visualize it in the form of a pact with the Devil. Only thus could they express the combination of fear and fascination which it inspired. Something similar happens in *The Merchant of*

Venice where a contract is signed at the beginning of the play between Antonio, a member of the new merchant class, and the Jew, conceived of as "the devil incarnal." This contract, which will disrupt the ivied peace of Belmont and its aristocratic inhabitants, will finally force us to acknowledge a new cash-nexus, a different concept of civil society, less feudal, less static than that of the Middle Ages, more dependent on individual private enterprise, energy and zeal. For this disturbing change in men's lives (actually the result of the rise of the new Puritan middle class) the Jew is held responsible. This is historically somewhat out of line, but there is no doubt of Shakespeare's historical intuition in representing this revolutionary change in the form of a contract or pact freely undertaken.

Fisch here anticipates the argument of Marc Shell, who points out that there are in this play no pure terms by which we can distinguish the bonds of monetary exchange from those that shape other human relations. The logic of exchange, with its codification of substitution and loss, is central to the conduct of business in Venice but also frames the logic of both legal punishment and redemptive sacrifice, the need for a victim who will pay back the debt incurred by humans in the Fall. Christian law, Shell writes, allows "for the commensurability of purses and persons"—or at least the play insists that this must be so. Shell indeed sees the logic of exchange and substitution at the heart of all literary language, the source of its power to generate metaphor, symbol, and plot; words work like coins in providing "ideological links between thought and matter, or between shadowy symbols and substantial things." Each face of exchange and all bonds that seek to order those exchanges—monetary, legal, erotic, and spiritual—are linked to the others in ways the play can never fully acknowledge. To that degree the idea of commerce shapes the play not through providing a reductive ground of human life, but rather through its unacknowledged dementia, through what it reveals about the world's organization around unstable and often invisible principles of exchange and lack. Lancelot's joke to Jessica, that her conversion to Christianity is dangerous because it will drive up the price of pork, is not trivial. In such a world, the blessed loss of self idealized in marriage, its ritualizing of the idea of perfect reciprocity, can also look like the institutionalizing of self-hatred, a bartering of life for life, a form of mutual enslavement, even a mutual suicide pact. Here even marriage comes under the auspices of the *lex talionis*. This entanglement of bonds means that no single bond can ever quite be canceled or redeemed by any other, though that is what absolutists like Shylock and Portia want. In a play where "the nature of the marriage bond and of human bondage in general" are relentlessly explored, we find at the heart of things a sense that the logic of exchange itself can never be transcended. At the close of the trial, for example, when Antonio himself claims the defeated Shylock's money "in use," Shell sees a scandalous leveling of value. We get only "two gelded users of money" face to face. "That the Jew is strained to become a merciful Christian and that the Christian becomes a kind of usurer are two signs that the Venetian court cannot provide a satisfactory resolution to the ideological dilemmas of property and person that gave rise to the action of *The Merchant of Venice* in the first place."

Exchange, as Shell sees it, is part of the texture of the human world, relentlessly bound up with the processes of thought and signification. What causes trouble is the need rigidly to measure, fix, or name the logic of exchange, since such an effort can depend only on blindness and, inevitably, coercion. Mere hatred of money in this sense entails a hatred of the world. What is dangerously seductive is the idea that money can crystallize or formalize the inevitable intersections of substance and lack in human life, and somehow manage to resolve all other systems of exchange or value. This illusion is linked to the somewhat different fantasy that monetary exchange can become the master trope of exchange itself. Such illusions are what make money in the play into a kind of golem, lending it a power to be both dead and alive, not merely a false god but a demon both real and unreal, a solvent of time, possibility, and desire, a defense against the realities of hazard and chance and time. That is part of its privative power, as Karl Marx brought out in his analysis of commodity fetishism. This is why money can produce a world in which prodigality takes the place of charity. The force of the play, for Shell, is that it exposes such errors even as it provides us with no easy means to solve them. He focuses our attention on the endless, dangerous shapes of exchange in the play, pointing to its larger lessons about the systems we use to reason about the world; he reminds us of how much the economic is structured even into the theological. That is Shell's power as a critic, to make us feel the intimate strangeness of the play's treatment of riches. He can make it clear why the play's concerns with money inevitably get tangled up with ideas about sacrifice and love, showing how this is part of the daily shape of language in Venice, even if we try to separate out the different realms or place them for security's sake in separate conceptual caskets.

What one misses in Shell is a responsiveness to that aspect of Shylock that resists translation even into so resonant a philosophical parable. One misses in him an ear for the singularity of Shylock's dramatic voice, a sense of Shylock's opacity rather than his symbolic transparency. That is what must also link Shylock to the singularity of Shakespeare and his dramatic economies. Shell loses both the specificity of Shylock's character and the specificity of the *artistic* economy in which he plays a role. That is why a consideration of the theatrical aspect of the work plays so little part in Shell. This is something that breaks the bounds of a sociological condition, and it cannot be universalized (as Shell wants to do) into a metaphysical condition. One thing that we need to think more about here is the quality of Shylock's emergent attachment to his bond, his knowing, eventually self-destructive dependence on this legal instrument; he asks it to enact an impossible exchange, to negotiate a compensation he knows cannot be accomplished. What we need to consider is his knowing, hallucinatory embrace of an error, his attempt to make the bond serve such extreme psychic and dramatic ends. He takes up or is taken up by the idea of his bond to the point that he speaks of it almost as the sole cipher of his identity and the sole vehicle of his agency in the world. It is a void into which all other significations fall.

I'll have my bond, I'll have no speaking, I'll have my bond, let them not speak but only listen, let them be silent, they have paid their penny or their sixpence to see the play and they must for that money forfeit their voices as well as their souls. They must bind to me those secret thoughts that my words stir up, silent answers, unknown ideas called forth by accidents and sudden occasions, feeble rumors that shake their hearts. How would I find those hidden things if I wasn't bound to them, they are not to be predicted or presaged or owned or carried off. They are the forfeits and profits of a bond not to be undone or requited. I give them gifts they can never pay back, certainly not with money, nor with applause, there is no breath or clapping that can easily release me, whatever my Prospero says, for the magic is no magic after all, and I hate their breath like the reek of rotten fens. My Shylock will never come out onstage to say that his spells are "all o'erthrown," begging for mercy or pardon, for the gentle breath of those who hate him, those whose hate feeds his person and his will, a will that conjures them by means of terror, the best and most dangerous of contracts, not to be counted, not to be summed. Neither I nor Shylock will ask from you a prayer on our behalf. Who would know how to pray for us?

Chapter Six

SHYLOCK UNBOUND

Shylock Three thousand ducats, well.

Bassanio Ay, sir, for three months.

Shylock For three months, well.

Bassanio For the which, as I told you, Antonio shall be bound.

Shylock Antonio shall become bound, well.

Bassanio May you stead me? Will you pleasure me? Shall I know your answer?

Shylock Three thousand ducats for three months, and Antonio bound.

From the very first moments of its being broached in the play, the question of the bond is linked to Shylock's habit of verbal repetition. We can approach the matter of the bond through looking initially at this aspect of Shylock's speech, in which he makes his own the most basic of poetic schemes. Repetition becomes, paradoxically, one mark of his singularity, crucial to the building up of his peculiar idiom or dramatic idiolect, as Otto Jespersen suggests. It gives form to an eloquence increasingly mysterious, unanswerable, and self-consuming, an eloquence that starts to undo more rational or harmonious pictures of the work or place of eloquence.

The lines quoted above mark Shylock's entry into the play's action, in act 1, scene 3. This is where he starts into our consciousness and into our ears. As we encounter his speech at this moment, Shylock's repetitions carry a comic note, as if he were dumbly echoing what others say. They also seem part of a calculated game. Shylock is playing dumb, taunting Bassanio by repeating his words yet refusing the answer they demand. He is, throughout the play, a great refuser of answers. Shylock may be even be inviting Bassanio himself to weigh more carefully what it is he asks of the moneylender. As John Gross points out, the repetitions have in them something of the accountant's manner of summing up the world, telling over its profits and losses, its risks, its currencies, its rates: "But ships are but boards, sailors but men; there be land rats, and water rats, water thieves and land thieves—I mean pirates" (1.3.18–20). You might even say that the repetitions reflect a certain poverty or miserliness of language, a thrifty reuse of formulas that have served him before. It suggests Shylock's pleasure in hearing his own words, a pleasure not unrelated to what we will see is his habit of ventriloquizing others' voices through his own, reinvesting them for his own rhetorical profit. There is something starker at stake as well. Shylock repeats words as a stay against chaos, and as a way of resisting solicitations he knows are either empty or opportunistic. So, when Bassanio invites him to dinner, he responds, "I will buy with you, sell with you, talk with you, walk with you, and so following; but I will not eat with you, drink with you, nor pray with you" (28–30). He uses repetition to mark out the area of what he cannot or will not share, the domain of those differences he himself is master of, as opposed to those (all too many) that the structure of Christian reality removes from his control. His social parsimony goes along with a decided isolation, since there are so few other persons in the play, it seems, with whom he will eat, drink, and pray. (Later, when he does go to eat with the Christians, it is to "feed" on them and impoverish them more.)

The stakes of repetition deepen in Shylock's most famous speech. Its claims on us lie in how it pushes repetition to structure a violent picture of sameness:

I am a Jew. Hath not a Jew eyes? Hath not a Jew hands, organs, dimensions, senses, affections, passions? Fed with the same food, hurt with the same weapons, subject to the same diseases, healed by the same means, warmed and cooled by the same winter and summer as a Christian is? If you prick us, do we not bleed? If you tickle us, do we not laugh? If you poison us, do we not die? And if you wrong us, shall we not revenge?

One may wonder what particular abuses he is trying to remember in such repetitions, and what, at the same time, such repetitions allow him to forget or dissolve into generality. Scholars have sometimes taken these lines, for all of their human urgency or homely eloquence, to manifest the automatism of the comedic villain; they become a sign of Shylock's reducing himself to a robot or animal, even at the moment when he claims his humanity. There is indeed a relentless, privative logic in that insistent formula, naturalizing revenge: "X us, do we not Y?" It is Shylock's way of making a stand, a way of holding off the prepossession of meaning by those he hates. He uses repetition as a way of refusing their automatic separation of Christian and Jew, miming that automatism, even as he tries to bridge the huge, unspeakable gap between Jew and Christian ("us" and "you") that the Christian world throws in his face. One aim of this is to make the word "Christian" as fraught, as little to be taken for granted, as the word "Jew," to refuse any prefabricated certainties about its scope, or about how the two words make sense through difference and opposition. Here we might think of a question that Ludwig Wittgenstein poses in *Philosophical Investigations*: "What would be missing . . . if you did not feel that a word lost its meaning and became a mere sound if it was repeated ten times over?" Shylock's way of courting such meaninglessness takes place in a world where apparently meaningful words are saturated with idiocy, cruelty, and mere pretense of meaning. A certain kind of strangeness has been stripped from us and must be restored exactly through repetition. The source of the speech's power, indeed, lies in its attempts to master a humanness that always slips from intelligibility, held there if at all by words that only pretend to define it. And yet, if we have ears to hear, Shylock's rhetorical questions are also real questions. "Hath not a Jew eyes? Hath not a Jew hands, organs, dimensions, senses, affections, passions?" What does it mean to be given these things, or simply to have them, as facts of the body and facts of the mind, facts about one's relation to the world, one's way of taking in, shaping, and being shaped by the world? It is everything and nothing. The power of these questions, and the frightening scope of the Jew's passions and "affections," will be made all the more visible in the trial scene, where Shylock in fact chillingly embraces the idea of his own automatism.

I have spoken already about the lines that follow in this scene, Shylock's mourning curse on Jessica, his inverted epitaph:

Why there, there, there, there! A diamond gone cost me two thousand ducats in Frankfurt! The curse never fell upon our nation till now, I never felt it till now. Two thousand ducats in that, and other precious, precious jewels! I would my daughter were dead at my foot, and the jewels in her ear: would she were hearsed at my foot, and the ducats in her coffin. . . . Why thou loss upon loss—the thief gone with so much, and so much to find the thief.

Here Shylock's words seek to frame and master loss exactly in repeating it, drawing it within a fantasy of compensation, reversal, revenge, and repossession. Repetition is a cipher of his melancholy, his sadness—which is partly the sadness of the cataloger or accountant who tries to balance a ledger of impossible debts and credits, losses and gains. Shylock tries to master loss by making it readable, making legible the wound and scandal of Jessica's betrayal.

Knowing exactly what is lost is part of the problem here. The repetitions themselves are a cipher of the labor of both remembering and putting away a memory, though we cannot tell what vision of his child, of earlier love or hatred, this entails. The loss of meaning is part of what is at stake here; it marks the dropping out of sense as well as of persons from the world. How much does Shylock understand his own loss of intelligibility? (How much does he take pleasure in it?) Here, at least, it seems unconscious, though he will later manipulate such a loss of sense in the trial scene, letting it be multiplied even as his gold and silver multiply; there he shows himself as a profiteer of loss, revealing the larger figurative implications of his career as usurer, only in that career's collapse. There is a triumph too in Shylock's wish. The repetitions join revenge with mourning, aggressively embedding the lost object within a larger system of losses as if to outwit a loss he cannot control. His attraction to such meaninglessness as Wittgenstein describes is at once a weakness and strength, something that he would own for himself and something that mirrors the world which so strips him of possessions.

There is perhaps an allusive aspect to Shylock's repetitions as well. Shakespeare invites us to hear in them echoes of the iterative modalities of biblical poetry. Such an association is in line with something I'll discuss below, the playwright's attempt to connect Shylock with the patriarchal narratives of the Old Testament, linking him to Abraham, Isaac, and Jacob, to the prophets, and even to Yahweh himself. The force of biblical parallelism can be exemplified by some triumphant lines from the song of Deborah, describing the humiliating death of the Philistine king Sisera at the hands of Jael, who pierces him through the temples with a tent stake while he sleeps: "He bowed him downe at her fete, he fel downe, & lay stil: at her fete he bowed him downe, and fel: and when he had sonke downe, he lay there dead" (Judges 5:27). If there is something sacral, even prophetic, in Shylock's curse that is reinforced by its echo of biblical cadences, we must yet see that Shakespeare has lent to such utterances a decidedly human, dramatic genealogy; he reminds us that such repetitions reflect the psychic and moral situation of this particular Jew, rather than lending his words a necessary sacrality. Shylock seems to recall the lines from Judges quoted above in his description of Jessica being buried at his feet. But if so, it is only to reinterpret and reverse the vision displayed in the biblical source, resisting what he must feel to be his own abject collapse at the feet of his Christianized daughter (who pierces his heart rather than his head). Equally biblical in its rhythm, and equally particular in its moral drama, is the bitter chiasmus of Shylock's complaint, "the thief gone with so much, and so much to find the thief," with its nuanced wordplay on the two shades of "so much."

The crisis of the play comes when news of Antonio's failed ventures puts the merchant into the hands of moneylender. Shylock suddenly discovers that his "merry bond"—which had begun as little more than a sly trick, or a way of shaming the merchant who mocked him—has teeth. It will feed his revenge. This discovery is also what provokes the most extreme example of Shylockian repetition in the play, just after the scene in Belmont where Bassanio wins Portia and the pair receive from Antonio the letter describing his peril. Right on the heels of this scene, we come to a very brief interlude. We see Shylock walking through the streets of Venice with Antonio in the custody of an officer, one whom, we must surmise, Shylock himself has hired to put his creditor under arrest. Despite his being in charge, however, Shylock is curiously nervous, fretful about exposure, about the officer's having brought the prisoner into the open air, as if Antonio were liable to be kidnapped by his fellow Christians as Jessica had been. The first words of this scene are Shylock's: "Jailer, look to him, tell me not of mercy" (3.3.1). We must assume that he speaks in response to some unheard plea for sympathy or mercy, a plea that the jailer had uttered in the moment just before their entrance and that we now infer only in its being silenced. (As it happens, the jailer says nothing at all in this scene, Shylock's one success in imposing silence.) Shylock's refusal to listen to any pleas against his case continues in the lines that follow, when Antonio takes up the argument:

Antonio Hear me yet, good Shylock—
Shylock I'll have my bond, speak not against my bond;
          I have sworn an oath that I will have my bond.

          .   .   .   .

Antonio I pray thee hear me speak—
Shylock I'll have my bond; I will not hear thee speak;
          I'll have my bond, and therefore speak no more.
          I'll not be made a soft and dull-eyed fool,
          To shake the head, relent, and sigh, and yield
          To Christian intercessors. Follow not!
          I'll have no speaking, I will have my bond. *Exit*   (3.3.3–17)

Let me digress for a moment, to mention an argument of Charles Spinosa, to the effect that Shylock's intimate attachment to his bond in this play evokes a medieval idea of contract that was itself under attack in the late sixteenth century—an ironic association, given the frequent linking of Jewish moneylenders with the depredations of modern commerce. This older idea of contractual bond depended less on the guaranteeing of profit and more on the wish of the signatories to build and explore existing communal relationships. It defines, Spinosa argues, a form of contract that can never quite explain itself; it is like a skill whose nature "is not to get behind and justify itself. It speaks not *about* itself, but *out of* itself," since its meanings are embedded in a texture of broader social dependences, needs, and charities, rather than being so strictly tied to the narrower purities of commerce. Such an idea of contract finds itself increasingly replaced by the arbitrariness and hyperrationalism of modern contract law, which considers the actions of people as implicitly containing discrete mental intentions that may be quantified and relied upon (and brought to trial when they are not fulfilled). Shylock, Spinosa suggests, has undertaken his bond not out of simple calculation. Rather, he had proposed his "merry bond," so literally bound to the body of his antagonist, as "a good way to explore and deepen his bitter relations with Antonio." The suggestion is attractive. Yet if the older idea of a legal bond survives here, it is disturbingly transformed; it points to the self-wounding and malicious impulses behind "exploring" a social relationship, even as it begins to include within itself the motive for profit, though profit of an uncanny sort. The bond in the end only isolates Shylock further, from himself as well as others. Hence its association in his mind with the power *of* silence and the power *to* silence.

Shylock's repetitions in this scene remind G. Wilson Knight of Aeschylus's Erinyes, "who are impervious to argument and similarly repeat themselves." We here get our first real look at the impenetrable Shylock as he appears at the trial. In his cutting off of pleas for mercy even at the start of things, Shylock seems, curiously, to be speaking to himself as much as to others. He is trying to keep down doubts of his own, even as he tries preemptively to silence the cries of "Christian intercessors" who would make of him a comic puppet of mechanical mercy, "to shake the head, relent, and sigh and yield." "I'll have my bond, and therefore speak no more. . . . I'll have no speaking, I will have my bond." The earlier repetitions of "Antonio bound" have come closer to home. To have his bond is to have no speaking about mercy. The bond has become his one secure possession, all that is left him in lieu of daughter and ducats—indeed, the means to recompense their loss. It is the cipher of his power and place, the one thing in which the law guarantees him property, or profit that is not usurious. The bond at this point becomes for Shylock the solvent of all meaning, the best answer to all others' speaking, showing the shape of his knowledge of himself and the danger he puts himself in. "My bond" is what he has, what he wills, what he says, the sufficiency of Shylock's hearing even. He is bound to his bond even more than Antonio is. It is almost the only word he needs, the last best gift he possesses. There is a curious kind of a dementia in his speech. The bond is now the form of Shylock's identity as well as a legal tool. As he speaks the word it acquires the air of a vulnerable piece of magic, a fragile spell. This bond, this contract, is the single thing that ties his private resentment to an impersonal public authority and that gives him a claim on the ear of the world, on its laws, even as it silences other voices, other claims, other knowledge or fears within himself (even, perhaps, his own impulses toward mercy). The bond speaks silence. Shylock points to it as a thing that stands in lieu of any other speech—having this bond means that, as he says to his Christian enemies at the trial, "I am not bound to please thee with my answers" (4.1.65). This contract is the one aspect of his identity which has *not* been imposed on him against his will, something other than that limiting, vicious and coercive gift of an identity over which he has no control, the one he inherits with his tribe and his profession, constituted by Christian hatred. The bond becomes an almost prophetic promise, a covenant, "*my* bond" now—"by our holy Sabaoth have I sworn / To have the due and forfeit of my bond" (36–37). He creates out of his bond a mystery, but also a fate. It is his daimon and his destiny (hence the rapidity of the collapse that follows Portia's tearing it away from him). Shylock in his focus on the bond stands for "hazard" raised to the position of a metaphysical principle.

Shylock makes repetition his own here. The very elusiveness of its individuating power is part of its claim on us. Shylock's repetitions touch on something that shatters any narrow boundaries of self or desire or possession, without losing an idiosyncratic gestural force. This vast expansion of the stakes of so common a formal device is almost a Shakespearean signature. We start to see the process by which, as R. P. Blackmur observes, Macbeth's "Tomorrow and tomorrow and tomorrow" or Lear's "Never never never never never" can show us "simple repetition metamorphosing the most familiar words into the most engulfing gesture." (Blackmur also adduces those repetitions of the word "will" in some of the later sonnets, where "the resultant meaning has nothing to do with will, but is an obsessive gesture of Shakespeare the man himself, made out of the single iterated syllable intensified into a half-throttled cry." We might bring up the further example of Mad Tom's "O, do, de, do, de, do, de," an iterative babble that choruses with the noise of the storm.) Other characters in *The Merchant of Venice* use repetition, of course. Portia employs it to moving effect in the scene quoted earlier, where she gives up herself and her fortune to Bassanio. Antonio uses iteration to answer Shylock's nonresponse to the judge's demand for an answer, insisting that there is no way to reason with so unreasonable a heart as the Jew's: "You may as well go stand upon the beach / And bid the main flood bate his usual height; / You may as well use question with the wolf / Why he hath made the ewe bleat for the lamb; / You may as well forbid the mountain pines / To wag their high tops and to make no noise" (4.1.71–76). Repetition also structures the duet of Lorenzo and Jessica in act 5, as they send forth variations on the theme of "In such a night . . ." Yet these repetitions have a different character. If they are not entirely parasitic upon Shylock's mode of repetition, they cannot match its increasingly stark, paradoxical eloquence. The words of Shylock show us an impulse at work in repetition which other characters do not know, a terror or a blankness of wish which their attempts at order cannot bear to acknowledge.

Chapter Seven

ARE YOU ANSWERED?

In the trial scene, Shylock displays a real ambition to command the proceedings, to make the court his own theater. In the way he pursues his legal case against Antonio, laying claim to the strict terms of his bond, I always feel an unsettling, willful sort of magic. It suggests a violent, Faustian despair—or, perhaps, a Faustian desire to remake the world according to his own wishes combined with a contempt, like that of Marlowe's Barabas, the Jew of Malta, for all values that claim to give the world shape and meaning. Shylock does not work secretly through poison, policy, or intricate trickery, as Marlowe's vengeful Jew does, as Jews were commonly said to work. Instead, he adopts an eerier, breathless kind of legal magic in which, as much as possible, nothing is hidden, in which he asks the impersonal powers of the law do his work for him (rather than taking the law into his own hands as a revenger would, since Shylock discovers that the law itself seems ready to give him the life he seeks). He releases the furies of the law even as he becomes himself a fury. It is difficult to describe the candor and incandescence of Shylock's stance, his frightening charisma, the way he magnetizes the courtroom even as he stands as an object of scorn. The scene puts him in a paradoxical situation. Shylock is at once terribly exposed and histrionically opaque; he puts on display his own opacity in his refusal to answer, allowing his motives, his very identity, to disappear into a radical insistence on the blank claims of the legal bond. The scandalous, surreal unknowableness of Shylock's motives, the inaccessibility of what he thinks, strikes others onstage too, as is audible in the Venetian Duke's wary words at opening, words that even he himself cannot believe: "Shylock, the world thinks, and I think so too, / That thou but lead'st this fashion of thy malice / To the last hour of act, and then 'tis thought / Thou'lt show thy mercy and remorse more strange / Than is thy strange apparent cruelty" (4.1.17–21). It is a cruelty that cannot be measured by whatever aspects of the Jew's character or secret intentions the Venetians think they already comprehend. Later in the trial scene Portia will assign this malice a narrower meaning, one that makes it punishable under the law, but for now it retains its ambiguity.

Shylock says almost nothing in the trial scene about his daughter's betrayal or the theft of his gold, nor does he rehearse the history of his being abused as Jew and usurer. He has buried away any claims on family or money or race or religion, even memory. The bond itself has become the cipher or ground of his identity, silencing other voices. Asked why he pursues his suit, he explains himself to the court only at the knowing expense of his own claims to being thought reasonable, to being read as an answerable human being. He insists, with a kind of wild humor, that his malice is only an occult impulse of the nerves, mere natural accident or hazard. He proves his own heartlessness:

> What if my house be troubled with a rat,
> And I be pleased to give ten thousand ducats
> To have it baned? What, are you answered yet?
> Some men there are love not a gaping pig;
> Some that are mad if they behold a cat;
> And others when the bagpipe sings i'the nose

Cannot contain their urine: for affection
Masters oft passion, sways it to the mood
Of what it likes or loathes. Now for your answer:
As there is no firm reason to be rendered
Why he cannot abide a gaping pig,
Why he a harmless necessary cat,
Why he a woollen bagpipe, but of force
Must yield to such inevitable shame
As to offend, himself being offended:
So can I give no reason, nor I will not,
More than a lodged hate and a certain loathing
I bear Antonio, that I follow thus
A losing suit against him. Are you answered?　　　(4.1.44–62)

Repetition, again, serves his purposes, becoming ever more unsettling in its effects, now turned against others. It is hard to know what's at stake in this refusal to explain himself, hard to describe its bite and improvisatory verve. (John Gross writes of the speech that it is indeed "hard to believe that it did not simply 'come' to Shakespeare, straight from his own unconscious.") In his earlier speech, "I am a Jew," Shylock had appealed to a radical transparency of mirroring motives, a sense that Jews and Christians work according to the same universal laws of human response, even in becoming inhuman. That outcry presses his listeners—if they have ears to hear—to test the limits of their own claims to humanity. In the "gaping pig" speech, Shylock says nothing about Jews or Christians, or even humans in general, only "some men"; he appeals to an animal-like aberrance, a grotesque automatism that seems by turns both human and inhuman. It is at best a parody of moral self-accounting.

Reading these lines, with their passionate heaping up of homely exemplars of inexplicability, I always hear a version of Montaigne's strategy of argument in "An Apology for Raymond Sebond." Shylock's reasoning about unreason offers a bizarre translation of the means by which Montaigne traces the radical limits of our understanding—in particular, his way of cataloging the many forms of human and animal behavior, even their most ordinary ranges of action and feeling, about whose logic we know nothing certain, subject as we are to the shifting powers of temperament, reason, fantasy, and language. (To cite one instance, in John Florio's 1603 translation: "I have seen some, who without infringing their patience, could not well heare a bone gnawne under their table: and we see few men, but are much troubled at that sharp, harsh, and teeth-edging noise that Smiths make in filing of brasse, or scraping of iron and steele together. . . . Nay, some will be angrie with, or hate a man, that either speaks in the nose, or rattles in the throat.") Montaigne undertakes his survey of intractable things with wonder, yet also to convince his readers, by appealing to such homely cases, to hold in doubt their own certainties about both human intentions and transcendental causes, and so hopefully forestall the cruelty such certainties can justify. ("I cruelly hate cruelty," he says, among all vices.) He invites a skepticism that takes in God as much as nature; it's an attempt to give over the self-destructive tyranny of our claims to knowledge. "We must become like the animals in order to become wise." In Shylock's case, however, any such merciful, tolerant, and Pyrrhonistic skepticism as we find in Montaigne is invoked to defend, even if it cannot quite explain, his cruel prosecution of Antonio; he is eerily uninterested in explanations that might win him sympathy. Perhaps he evades rational explanation, such as the law asks of him, so as not to sound crazy to himself. Yet it is at the cost of making himself sound crazy to others. He is not even a fanatic of the law here, like Heinrich von Kleist's Michael Kohlhaas, who faces down all authority in seeking compensation for theft. The sequence of Shylock's comparisons is stunning. Think first of that "gaping pig," an unclean creature with which Shylock for a moment seems to identify himself, an object of "some men's" loathing and others' appetite. Even if he is referring to a roasted pig, its mouth fixed open by the oven, the word "gaping" makes the thing seem half-alive, staring or taking in air, almost astonished. Then think of the rat-catching cat that makes some men mad. Shylock is both cat and rat, as is Antonio. Finally, listen to how Shylock describes the person who cannot bear the sound of a bagpipe. Such a man is one who "of force / Must yield to such inevitable shame, / As to offend, himself being offended." This curiously inverts Lorenzo's account in act 5 of music's power to pacify or humanize wild animals. Shylock's words suggest that the man he describes, unable to contain his urine at the bagpipe's whine, is somehow content knowingly to piss himself in public in order to express his own offense at the offensive sound. This reads to me as Shylock's half-voiced account of his own situation: to offend, himself being offended. Shylock thus implicitly acknowledges something of his own shame, humiliation, and terror in this scene, his willful abandonment of human dignity and answerability in the process of making his revenge "inevitable." The idea of self-offense is the clearer in the first quarto text of the play (1600), which omits the comma often supplied by modern editors after "offend" in order for the line to read "to offend, himself being offended." The quarto has rather "to offend himself being offended," inviting us to understand "himself" as the direct object of "to offend," thus folding together more ambiguously offense at others and self-offense.

Shylock's argument, his posture of rage and resentment, can feel curiously vulnerable, both in what he gives voice to and in what he keeps silent about. It is hard to say if Shylock himself knows exactly what satisfaction he seeks in the courtroom, hard to know not simply what he thinks but what he is feeling. Does he know how this imaginary cut will answer his real losses? Does he know what he will cut at all? How does he imagine, and ask us to imagine, what it will be like to touch Antonio's skin with his knife, that blade which he whets, as vicious Gratiano says truly enough, "not on thy sole, but on thy soul"? (What, after all, do we imagine is in Abraham's mind as he prepares to drive his knife into his son's throat? What terror, hope, or sense of witness? It is that order of mystery I feel brought into play in the trial scene.) Does Shylock understand that the wording of the bond has unaccountably shifted from a pound of flesh "to be cut off and taken / In what part of your body pleaseth me"—as in act 1—to a pound of flesh to be cut off from "nearest [the merchant's] heart"—as Portia reads it? Shylock, who elsewhere makes one so strongly feel the uncanny animation of inanimate substances, here makes himself the most aggressively uncanny of creatures. In the "gaping pig speech," especially, he makes what desperate resistance he can, as Stanley Cavell suggests, to the influx of powerful doubts about the scope of his own humanness, a skepticism that catches us as well.

In his essay "Freedom and Resentment," P. F. Strawson reflects on those offensive acts that may induce us to suspend our natural resentment against the persons committing them, which means holding aloof from assuming that such acts are the result of free will or choice, and hence accessible to both our condemnation and our feelings of moral offense. These are often cases in which we say of a person who has done something injurious that "he didn't mean it" or "he couldn't help it," when we say that he was temporarily or permanently "not himself," usually because that person is a child, a maniac, in a temporary fit, or on drugs. We can slip into this attitude, suspending our resentment, without necessarily suspending our disgust, rage, embarrassment, and bafflement at the act itself. Such an "objective position" in relation to a source of offense "may include repulsion or fear, it may include pity or even love, though not all kinds of love. But it cannot include the range of reactive feelings and attitudes which belong to involvement or participation with others in inter-personal human relationships; it cannot include resentment, gratitude, forgiveness, anger, or the sort of love which two adults can sometimes be said to feel reciprocally, for each other." Objective attitudes such as Strawson describes "do not invite us to view the *agent* as one in respect of whom [our reactive attitudes] are in any way inappropriate. They invite us to view the *injury* as one in respect of which a particular one of these attitudes is inappropriate." As he points out, in such cases of suspended moral reaction we do something like what a determinist does, but in a way that makes sense only if we allow the larger complexities of human relationships, something that demands a constant shift or compromise between "participant" and "objective" attitudes. To assume an objective attitude thus serves us as a moral resource; it is a position that we occupy temporarily and that is subject to a continual revision of judgment, judgment that changes depending on what we know about the person we judge. Of a person whose nature causes us to suspend moral resentment against his acts, or to say "he didn't mean it," Strawson writes, "You cannot quarrel with him, and though you may talk to him, even negotiate with him, you cannot reason with him. You can at most pretend to quarrel, or to reason, with him."

Strawson's larger project, undertaken very much in the spirit of Wittgenstein, is to explore the language games that belong to philosophical determinism, and to see their family resemblance to other gestures, positions, and stances of philosophical explanation. Determinism becomes intelligible to him only in relation to a larger set of practices and judgments. His essay drives toward the conclusion that the ineluctable nature or quality of human resentment entails a suspension of the possibility of determinism. We only truly resent persons whose offense is the product of free choice. Resentment is thus, ironically enough, a guarantor of our freedom of will and of our embeddedness in a structure of human relations. However dangerous some of its forms may be, our feeling of resentment suggests our commitment to something beyond determinism (though Strawson also goes on to criticize any opposing version of "free will" that too readily abandons "the thickly entangled forest of human moral relations and judgements.")

What is particularly unsettling about the "gaping pig" speech, seen in relation to Strawson, is that Shylock invokes a kind of moral determinism that masks, even as it seeks to deny, the rawer claims of resentment; he happily invokes a dehumanized position for himself (as well as for the object of his resentment), yet in a way that both strengthens his hatred and renders it uncanny. He refuses to point to more intelligible human causes or rationales; he refuses a calculus of reason as much as he refuses a calculus of mercy. That is partly because the Christians' demand for mercy asks him to be part of an ethical community from which he knows himself to be excluded. They ask him to commit a singular act of mercy that is not answered by, or answerable to, a larger community of mercies. Shylock is asked to be merciful in a way that doesn't acknowledge the scope of what mercy he could truly offer. He sees that he is asked to be merciful toward one who has contempt for his mercy, partly because his mercy would spare the court from having to bear the consequences of Antonio's folly or to plumb the mysteries of Shylock's malice. Mercy on another's terms Shylock cannot provide, even if he could provide it on his own. Instead, he affronts mercy in a way that holds mercy up to judgment, suggests its opportunism and hypocrisy, its rawer contingency (rather than its heavenly gratuitousness). He puts claims for mercy and forgiveness to the test just by making himself so terribly unforgivable; he is as unforgivable as he is unforgiving, refusing the coercions of forgiveness, choosing against its seductive economy or profit (being as it is, in Portia's words, "twice blessed"). He refuses, you could say, a commerce of mercy—the two words are indeed linked etymologically, "mercy" deriving from Latin *merces*, "wages," "fee," or "recompense," a word that shares a root with Latin *merx*, "commodity" or "goods," the source of "commerce," whence also Mercury, god of traders, thieves, and tricksters. Shylock, like Melville's vengeful Ahab, has here set himself beyond any rational calculation, rejecting any fear that the real cost of pursuing what he himself calls "a losing case" might be greater than its imaginary gain. The court asks of him an isolated mercy and yet refuses him what Strawson calls "vicarious" mercy: "In general, though within varying limits, we demand of others for others, as well as of ourselves for others, something of the regard which we demand of others for ourselves."

This is, roughly, the basis of Shylock's bitter claim in his "I am a Jew" speech. At the trial, things change. Shylock there adapts a deterministic thesis in regard to his own feelings of resentment; he stands outside himself, describing his own moral passion as automatic, deterministic, and compulsive, demanding implicitly that others suspend *their* resentment, for how could one resent so animal-like a hater? Shylock employs a demented sort of legalism here, one that parodies the suspension of interest or passion required by the law. He seems to give up his own claims to moral resentment, refuses himself, and thus others, the apparent justice of hatred. Hence his words' moral and conceptual shock. In Strawson's terms, one could say that Shylock invokes a universalizing suspension of sympathy that ordinarily would serve the uses of those in authority, those in control of the laws. Shylock makes himself a law unto himself. Is he thus exposing the inhumanity of the law, as well as his own inhumanity? Here you might consider Shylock's stance as resembling the kind of parabolic acts of self-degradation characteristic of Old Testament prophets, their way of making a scandal or enigma of themselves, as when Isaiah walks naked through the condemned city of Jerusalem or Ezekiel cooks his bread over dung and makes himself taboo. Shylock reminds us that there is a prophetic as well as idolatrous or sinful obstinacy, as in Isaiah: "I hid not my face from shame and spitting. . . . I shall not be confounded. . . . therefore have I set my face like a flint, and I knowe I shal not be ashamed" (50:6–7).

As many have felt, the scene shows us the Jew holding up to the Christians a mirror of their own hatred. It shows them an image of that hatred's contingency and ungroundedness rather than its reasonableness, its exemplarity. The mirror he offers here is different from the one implied by Shylock's earlier question about how he should react to being wronged by Christians—"What should [a Jew's] sufferance be by Christian example?"—which appeals to shared human standards of judgment, however misapplied. Shylock's embrace of idiosyncrasy indeed may call attention to the terror of idiosyncrasy and difference that is itself a source of anti-semitism. (I think here of the late medieval emblem of the *Judensau*, a monstrous, tusked sow ridden upon and sucked at by a crowd of bearded Jews, one of them invariably probing the creature's anus.) To what degree does he imply that his reaction should be universalized, extended to all cases? The problem of the Jew is the problem of particularity, the problem of selecting someone from within the human species to be the site of the inhuman. Yet Shylock's speech, in its hallucinatory logic, implies that to make a Jew into an animal ends up making the whole world bestial, making it not a human community but a herd, flock, or pack. How does a herd of goats choose a scapegoat for itself?

The trial scene also points to a theatrical as well as a moral or legal experiment, and here again we catch another side of what it means to say that Shylock is Shakespeare. Describing the prophetic force of Timon's and Shylock's implacability, their mocking rage at being asked for favor by the community that has scorned them, Knight insists that "it would be to lay too limited an emphasis on the fictional surfaces to fail to see in these dramas signs of poetic genius taking a mighty pleasure in putting the community in its place." That means keeping the audience in the theater rather than driving them out of it, inviting their shame, terror, and resentment instead of their indulgence or pardon—more fully, say, than in the spectacle of the self-pleasing villain Richard III.

Chapter Eight

A THEATER OF COMPLICITY

What looms up for me at the trial, for all of Shylock's reductiveness and aggression, his refusal of mercy, is a sense of his paradoxical generosity. Shylock's is a different kind of grace, more aggressively secular, both natural and unnatural. This is most apparent in his complex histrionics, the generosity of the actor or clown exposing his mask to the audience. He indeed employs in court a more extreme version of that self-dramatizing mockery which he had earlier turned against Antonio, during their first encounter in act I. There he showed himself to be what Lawrence Danson calls "an actor's actor," a creature in love with his own masks and powers of improvisation, even as he demonstrates his sharp ear for impulses that run below the surface of other people's words. Attacked for his usurious habits by the very merchant who seeks a loan from him, Shylock rehearses Antonio's history of abuse—"You call me misbeliever, cut-throat dog, / And spit upon my Jewish gaberdine"—and goes on to offer, in response, his own bitterly comic turn:

> Monies is your suit.
> What should I say to you? Should I not say

"Hath a dog money? Is it possible
A cur can lend three thousand ducats?" Or
Shall I bend low, and in a bondsman's key,
With bated breath and whisp'ring humbleness,
Say this:
"Fair Sir, you spat on me on Wednesday last,
You spurned me such a day, another time
You called me dog: and for these courtesies
I'll lend you thus much monies."   (1.3.111–21)

Shylock conjures up an image of himself as exactly the servile dog, slave, or bondsman the Venetians want him to be. We can even imagine that the actor playing Shylock mimes the very creature he says the Christian world makes of him, embracing what wounds him even as he steals for himself the shapes of its hatred. The mere word "dog" shines like rotten wood. (How does the word taste in his mouth?) This is a momentary game, but it speaks of ancient resources of bitterness and play in Shylock, mixed with stark knowledge of his old enemy, Antonio, who is provoked by these words into his most explicit expression of loathing: "If thou wilt lend this money, lend it not / As to thy friends . . . But lend it rather to thine enemy, / Who if he break, thou mayst with better face / Exact the penalty" (124–29).

The stakes of such a game change at the trial, however. In earlier scenes, Shakespeare shows us a Shylock who embodies the stereotypes of Jewish villainy only in a limited way, most prominently as he is reflected in the words of others. We catch the note of his preoccupation with money and thrift, his rage at being persecuted, and his desire to feed on those who hate him. Bassanio calls him a villain, Antonio a devil, as does Lancelot Gobbo in a comic vein, and the bored and amorous Jessica says his house is hell. But the full-blown monstering of the Jew we see in a play like *The Jew of Malta* is held back. In the Venetian court those stereotypes of Jewish menace break through more strongly, partly because Shylock, know-

ingly and willfully, takes them upon himself. He makes himself
into exactly the bloodthirsty, invidious, devilish, vengeful, doglike,
and scripture-wresting Jew that the Christians expect him to be.
And he does this not as a momentary comic improvisation in the
street, but nakedly at a public hearing, as part of the structure of
a legal ritual. Even as he refuses to yield to the Christians' persua-
sions, Shylock shows himself ironically as their creature, their cur,
the embodied form of their fears (including their hidden terror
at their own rage as it is directed at this imaginary monster). He
steals their projections for himself, wrests from their control the
very accusatory and defamatory mask that others had fitted upon
him. For the Venetians, this mask must seem an unmasking, the
showing forth of the deep truth about Jews. Yet Shylock makes the
face of Jewish malice more unsettling than they thought they knew
or could have imagined. In this scene, his posture becomes a place
where persecution and resistance meet. His is a mask formed from
both inside and outside, at once shield and punishment, wound and
weapon.

Shylock restores to us a sharp sense of the rage underlying such
masks; he makes such rage more strangely visible. That is part of
the logic of the scene, the source of its dramatic power. Shylock's
hatred is a mirror of Christian hatred; he shows that hatred in its
ferocity and its arbitrariness. Equally or more unsettling is that
his performance shows us the glee that can inform such postures
of hatred. He shows us their frightening pleasure, their gamesome-
ness. He suggests how such hatred, projected onto another, releases
the hater from his fear and anxiety about the self's and the world's
unknowable being. Shylock speaks to a pleasure and a freedom in
which victim and victimizer seem to be complicit. This mask is a
point of transit, something assumed and something imposed. What
I hear him saying to the Venetians at the trial is this: You want to
see a cutthroat dog, I'll show you a cutthroat dog. You want to see
legalism, I'll show you legalism. This is what Jewish hard-heart-
edness looks like. You want demonic malice, here it is. Shylock's

masking is a way of knowing both himself and his enemies at the same moment. It is a way of knowing the madness of the world he inhabits and its mad entertainments, knowing the blankness of its hatred and his own status as "the hated man." This is what I meant by Shylock's candor and incandescence; he unconceals himself even as he assumes so frightening a mask, or translates himself into a mask. These postures shape his presence for others onstage. They also show Shylock courting absence or invisibility in his recognition of how hollow such postures are, for all their virulence. Shylock's power in the scene comes partly from the paradoxical sense that he is not there at all. More than anything else, he reveals himself as a hallucination of the Christians, the focal point of their fear. Even as he is saying "You want to see this?" he knows that there's nothing to see.

One would like to think that the Venetians could take the lesson. That is optimistic. Shylock's indecorum, his way of at once refusing and accepting the terms of the Venetians, is too stark. They cannot see themselves in him. They cannot overhear their own hatred echoed back to them from Shylock any more than Prospero can hear in the curses of Caliban the vengeful echo of his own anxious curses against his recalcitrant slave. Indeed, what emerges in the trial scene may surprise even Shylock. Did he know that he could push so far the limits of the possible? Do we imagine him as astonished at what he has risked or what he has been allowed to say? The scene is a lesson, again, in the aesthetics of repugnancy. This repugnancy lies not in the mere ugliness of Venetian antisemitism but in Shylock's fierce embrace of things unaccountable or irresponsive to logical analysis. It inheres in his very theatricality, his way of turning this mask or face of monstrosity against the Venetians, binding them to him even as he refuses their demand for a reasonable regard.

There is a remarkable commedia dell'arte skit, or *lazzo*, as it is called, the text of which survives in a Neapolitan manuscript dated around 1700. It describes the bare bones of a scene that would have been much elaborated in live performance: "Pulcinella, in desperate need of money, goes to borrow from the Jews. Informed that there are two rates of interest—a very high one for Gentiles and a lower one for Jews—Pulcinella decides to convert. The Jews gather around Pulcinella and start to circumcise him." We can only imagine what kind of comically menacing Jews, with papier-mâché noses, long knives, and red hats, surrounded Pulcinella, himself servant clown, long nosed and hunchbacked (a *gobbo*, in Italian), or what improvisations of need, bafflement, comic cruelty, and comic suffering the actors came up with. The scene suggests just how strangely the stage Jew, in all his menace, can be implicated in the comic world, how raw are the fears that are given shape and contained by that figure.

Both E. E. Stoll and C. L. Barber argue passionately, against the grain of a tragic reading of Shylock, that we should not overlook his generic role in the play as comic villain and comic scapegoat—combining elements the New Comedy types of the jealous, controlling *senex*, outwitted by the younger generation, and the upstart, cursing slave, mixed with specifically Jewish types of jeering and menace (familiar from the medieval mysteries). Stoll, who lays out starkly enough the antisemitic backgrounds of the play, insists on the "comparative hardness of heart" that comedy requires. One should not, he writes, waste the play's "harsh and vindictive laughter" in false sympathy (though he also speaks of a grotesqueness in Shylock that "passes over the border of laughter— perhaps of tears"). And Barber is eloquent in his argument that to see Shylock as a tragic victim, to neglect what the play shows of his viciousness and moral blindness, yields ground to a sentimentality about victims that has larger costs. He would remind us of how often victims are used to serve the watcher's needs, "to nourish self-esteem or control our own fears," as Judith Shklar writes. To the degree that such arguments are true, we must yet see that Shylock takes this generic role and turns it to his own purposes. He commands it, uses it to unsettle as well as indulge his audience. If Shylock is a clown, he also shows us the darker spaces of knowledge that the stage clown can open up. In particular, he shows us the power of the clown's relentless embrace of his own failure and humiliation, his way of making comic capital out of his wounded heart, out of his shame and vulnerability, which is the way of all clowns from Robert Armin to Charlie Chaplin. Shylock reveals the theatrical clown's peculiar complicity with the audience, his responsiveness to the theatrical occasion and its contingent needs. We are reminded of the clown's way of turning his audience's laughter back on itself, mocking viewers even as he mocks the artifices of theater at large, taking delight in them at the same time, improvising on them in the moment, balancing at the threshold of what is unscripted and unpredictable. Shylock's is a particularly harrowing version of the clown game. If he invites his audience's complicity, he also stops their laughter in their throats, shows them its costs. I am thinking of the moment at the trial when, virtual slave that he is, Shylock speaks with unexpected eloquence about the abject uses the Venetians make of their own slaves, inviting them to set the slaves free or marry them to their daughters. In his taunting of the Venetians, he must see that he exposes himself to the threat of real violence in return. We should perhaps think of this game as a conscious piece of theatrical exploration, as Shakespeare testing his dramatic means by prying open new spaces of possibility within the generic frame of comedy. In his book on Shakespearean comedy, *A Natural Perspective*, Northrop Frye writes, with Shylock very much on his mind, that "what fascinates us about the *idiotes* and clown is that they are not purely isolated individuals: we get fitful glimpses of a hidden world which they guard or symbolize. They may be able to speak for their world . . . or it may remain locked up in their minds, breaking through suddenly and involuntarily. . . . But it is never a wholly simple world." The clown guards that to which we are most vulnerable, as well as that in which we take most delight.

The Shylocks I have seen onstage—stoic, ironic, sorrowful, or angry—tried to keep audiences in view of a human Shylock, a Shylock who is vulnerable and who makes us vulnerable, one whose call for justice touches us, however frightening we find his plot against Antonio. They wanted, I suspect, a Shylock with analogies to Lear and Timon. I have never seen an actor capable of bearing fully the bitter humor of the part, ready to show himself at once wounded and elated by Shylock's rage, lifted up by his grotesque histrionics. For myself, I think that the greatest Shylock of the twentieth century would have been Zero Mostel. In part I am re-calling Mostel's performance in the 1974 film version of Eugène Ionesco's *Rhinoceros*, when he changes from a boisterous, officious, aggressively courtly friend of the hero into a snorting, raging ani-mal, taken over by an impulse that seems at once uncontrollable and curiously pleasurable, like a sneeze, something caught from the invisible infection of other human rhinoceroses popping up in the world of the play. But mostly I'm imagining a Shylock who would be a more ferocious version of Mostel's Max Bialystock in Mel Brooks's 1968 film *The Producers*, huge, louche, abject, mocking, contemp-tuous, restless, insinuating, shameless, and seductive. Bialystock is a man who swindles poor old ladies out of their life savings in order to fund an antisemitic farce that he knows will be a crashing failure, but that will thereby gain him an incalculable profit. He is a clown who succeeds ruinously, against his very will to fail, when the musical he produces, *Springtime for Hitler*, turns out to be a huge comic success—driven as it is, we come to see, by a generous anger against Nazi violence that the greedy, servile producer can barely acknowledge even to himself. Mostel would have invented for us a Shylock who ate his own and others' rage for breakfast. What you want, if only for a moment, is Shylock the maddened clown, one who gapes back at the gaping pig, who listens to that shrieking bagpipe and finds himself standing, shamelessly, with relish and knowledge, in his piss-soaked pantaloons and gaberdine. (Mostel did in fact get to play Shakespeare's moneylender onstage, but it was in Arnold Wesker's *Shylock*, a well-intentioned but forced reimagining of the original play, where Shylock is no monster but a philanthropic bibliophile, Antonio's best friend, in fact. The play contrives to have Antonio and Shylock, as well as Portia and Jessica, share at the end a tragic knowledge of the cruelty inflicted on all of them by Venetian law and prejudice. The actor died a few days after the play's preview in 1977, at the end of a trying course of rehearsals and rewritings, described in the playwright's absorbing memoir, *The Birth of Shylock and the Death of Zero Mostel.*)

The ambivalent lure of the clown shows us with a particular intensity the lure of the actor in general. A character like Shylock strikes us just because he evokes the metaphysical shock of acting, the actor's generosity and freedom, his aggression and vulnerability, his exposure to the audience's hatred as well as its love. This shock is evoked, as Michael Goldman makes very clear, in all of the great character roles written for the stage, from Sophocles' Oedipus to Beckett's Hamm. Shylock's postures grip us just because they so starkly mirror the energy of the actor's embrace of impulses which might shame both himself and his audience. The actor survives onstage by risking offense, himself being offended; he feeds on his own shame, his own ambivalent love and fear of making a spectacle of himself, his impulse to make himself a motley to the view. This risk is what gives the actor onstage the power to shame us and yet to make a gift or revelation out of that shame, even as the element of play helps to exorcise shame in its more divisive forms.

Shylock must somehow intend his ironic appropriation of masks, even if he cannot acknowledge it. Or, to put it another way, he releases a will to masking, a sense of masking's ambiguous uses and pleasures, lending to these the coloring of something unconscious, something that touches on more archaic, unowned sources of rage and fear. The power of the character lies in how Shylock, in the trial scene, happens to himself, as well as in how he happens to others. The old question of how human or tragic a figure Shakespeare has made his Jewish villain remains inescapable; it is not just a reversion to Victorian sentimentality. Yet the key to this question is that Shylock, as a piece of dramatic mimesis, takes much of his mysterious, compulsive, violent, and knowing interiority from the very language that seeks to strip him of his humanity. He takes his inner life from the very antisemitic mythmaking that would convert him into a grotesque puppet, a cipher of Christian resentment. Shakespeare has humanized Shylock exactly through as much as in spite of the alien mask fitted on his face. This process of translation or, better, excavation and theft, a process by which an equivocal blessing is stolen from a curse, is central to what I mean by Shylock's generosity. It is a generosity of hearing as much as speaking, insofar as it hinges on how we imagine Shylock taking in a whole world of antisemitic abuse, making of it a stranger endowment, an endowment that he shares with us and with the Venetians at the trial. If this transformation has something in it of the actor's and the clown's generosity, it also shows us the playwright's generosity as a creator of theatrical characters, especially as one who takes up and transforms within his play the inherited image of the murderous Jew, giving it a wholly unexpected inflection. This is not, again, a matter of softening the archetype, of making it more sympathetic or more pitiable. Shakespeare's way of entering into that tradition is indeed entirely pitiless, toward himself as well as others. Shakespeare's generosity is a pitiless generosity. Marlowe's Barabas, the Jew of Malta, is a Machiavel who both literally and figuratively heaps up "infinite riches in a little room," compassing more will, knowledge, and mastery than anyone else in his world. Yet however large his accumulations are, he can never keep within himself the elements of strangeness and vulnerability as Shylock does. Barabas remains a demonic puppet, without Shylock's baffling claim on our hearts.

A pitiless generosity. Yes, so he says. Shylock is me, Shamedseeker, Snakespier, Shyclock, Slyshock. What shakes me, laughter or fear? If I have made myself a clown, made myself a motley to the view, I will show the audience how much a clown can show, how much is gained in selling cheap what is most dear. I will put myself and Shylock to the test in this trial, I will raise up an enemy against him that will strip him even more than he strips himself and then I'll give him back some part of what he has lost. I will give it back to him as a curse such as Job could never have imagined, he who gets back his beautiful daughters and his riches twice over. Shylock will get things back in ways that leave him all the more a ghost. I want to survive as Shylock survives, as hatred survives, as curse survives, shared out amongst all of you who watch and listen. My Shylock strives to persist in time. We will survive as love of hatred and love in hatred, love secured by hatred even as hatred is secured by law. We survive through those who hate us as much as through those who love us. It is hard to hear, the music of this hatred, it is at once so fleshly and so spiritual a music. It is the noise of the world and the noise of clamoring hearts. What kind of hearts do you need to hear this music? Hearts of flesh that are as hard as stone. Is there any cause in nature that make these hard hearts? As long as men can breathe, and eyes can see, so long lives this. It is part of time, a gift to time, the noise of time that carries all away, stealing my children from under my nose, my flesh and blood, stealing my gold.

Chapter Nine

THE THIRD POSSESSOR

You are always looking for a possible Shylock, a face of life, something to face against life, able to match its mania, a creature whose
words transform our own. If you hold a mirror up to nature it will
sometimes show you the head of Medusa.

The energy of Shylock at the trial is frightening partly because
it is frighteningly hard to read. He so willfully empties himself
out, makes of himself a monster refusing human accountability. It
is his rigid isolation of appetite, its obsessiveness and its poverty—
despite what I called his arcane generosity—that makes Shylock
feel like a daimonic or allegorical agent, as Angus Fletcher has described such figures, resembling persons possessed by an idea, pris-
oners of meaning. In particular, Shylock makes himself a creature
that mirrors the Pauline idea of the Law. He fits Paul's idea of the
Law as an archaic trap, a stumbling block or *skandalon*, something
with a cunning power of its own to find out sin. Paul sees in the
Law a face of God that grounds the human situation, a principle
that creates sin yet has itself been superseded as a means of salvation. The Law is linked in turn to other insidious allegorical agents
or personifications, the Flesh, the World, Sin, the Synagogue, and
the Devil. As a double of what Paul calls the letter, referring to the

literal sense of the Old Testament, the Law points to the founding terms of Christian typological allegory itself, which opposes to the letter its own mechanisms of exegesis, grounded in the authority of the spirit. (The Law as letter is thus an allegorical picture of the enemy of allegory.) In this sense, Shylock represents the fascination of a true but transcended origin, as when, in his threat to have the heart out of Antonio, he mocks by literalization Paul's spiritualizing overgoing of Hebrew law in Romans 2:29, where Paul speaks of "the circumcision . . . of the heart." This is why, in more theological readings of *The Merchant of Venice*—going back to August Wilhelm Schlegel, and articulated most carefully by modern readers of the play such as Lawrence Danson, Anthony Hecht, and Barbara Lewalski—Shylock at trial simply is the Law, a figure of the Law's demonic literalism, its murderous, even self-destructive power, and its working of divine revenge against a nation which adheres to the Law without knowing its need for correction by the power of Mercy. This is a role that Portia will invite Shylock himself to take on in the trial scene, before she makes the law do a more local work of revenge, even as she steals for herself the mask of Mercy.

The play as a whole makes impossible any strictly Pauline reading of its dynamics. *The Merchant of Venice*, like many of Shakespeare's plays, reflects the poet's deep fascination with the dialectical mode of Paul's writing, his oppositional imagery, his framing of battles between opposed worlds, texts, persons, and churches. Shakespeare took from Paul lessons in the cunning reappropriation of traditions, studying as well Paul's way of locating himself at an equivocal threshold between conflicting domains, Jew and Christian, alien and cosmopolitan, citizen of this world and citizen of a world to come, as Julia Reinhard Lupton has suggested. The poet must have sensed the importance of Pauline thinking for the reformist logic of Protestant theology. If he echoes Paul's freedom of reading, he also complicates the factional or apocalyptic quality of Paul's thought, its spiritual absolutism, even as he shows his understanding of Paul as the most slyly opportunistic of writers. At moments, indeed, Shakespeare's use of Paul shows us the founder of Christianity as a poet of the mind's dream, one whose way of thinking is itself protean, often caught between conflicting occasions, aims, and languages. This is perhaps why the newly awakened Bottom in *A Midsummer Night's Dream*, in what remains the great touchstone for understanding Shakespeare's use of Paul, so mangles the eschatological oppositions of 1 Corinthians 2:9, turning "the eye hath not seen, & the eare hath not heard, neither have entred into the heart of man, the thynges which God hath prepared for them that love hym" (Bishop's Bible [1568]), into "the eye of man hath not heard, the ear of man hath not seen, man's hand is not able to taste, his tongue to conceive, nor his heart to report, what my dream was." In Shakespeare, Pauline typology is always mediated, held up for examination, its allusive underpinnings questioned, its silences given voice, and its dramatic logic laid bare. It points to a human subject for human drama.

The authoritative claims of Pauline typology are further tempered in *The Merchant of Venice* by the gravitational pull of Old Testament narrative, its literary and psychological density. One gets a sense that Shakespeare, unable to draw on any experience of actual Jews, but wanting more than the demonic puppets of Paul or antisemitic legend, fleshed out the human particulars of Shylock by studying closely the details of the patriarchal history in Genesis. These he probed, as M. M. Mahood subtly suggests, with the same eagerness that he studied the grittier, more idiosyncratic and anecdotal narratives of Plutarch in order to give a more local grounding, a human thickness, to his dramatizations of Roman history. The specificity of his engagements with the text of Genesis acts as a counterweight to any strictly allegorical reading of the play. This is clear in the early scene where Shakespeare lends to Shylock something of his own verve for reading the patriarchal history in all of its odd human drama. Responding to Antonio's denigration of profiting by usury, Shylock retells an episode from the story of Jacob, his ancestor and double:

When Jacob grazed his uncle Laban's sheep—
This Jacob from our holy Abram was
(As his wise mother wrought in his behalf)
The third possessor; ay, he was the third—

. . . .

. . . Mark what Jacob did:
When Laban and himself were compromised
That all the eanlings which were streaked and pied
Should fall as Jacob's hire, the ewes being rank
In end of autumn turnèd to the rams,
And when the work of generation was
Between these woolly breeders in the act,
The skilful shepherd pilled me certain wands
And in the doing of the deed of kind
He stuck them up before the fulsome ewes,
Who then conceiving, did in eaning time
Fall parti-coloured lambs, and those were Jacob's.
This was a way to thrive, and he was blest;
And thrift is blessing if men steal it not.   (1.3.63–82)

It is blessing even if they *do* steal it, he might add sotto voce. Antonio's response, though tellingly marked by the merchant's word "venture," is sufficiently orthodox: "This was a venture, sir, that Jacob served for, / A thing not in his power to bring to pass, / But swayed and fashioned by the hand of heaven" (83–85). The Geneva Bible's gloss reads, "Iaakob herein used no deceit: for it was Gods commandement as he declareth in [Genesis] 31:9, 11." But Shakespeare himself has felt his way into the text less apologetically. That of which Jacob is the third possessor, after Abraham and Isaac, is the divine blessing, though Shylock (intentionally or not) elides this. In Genesis, the blessing is very much bound to the world of time; it is a matter of children, descendants, servants, flocks, and land, the emergence of a nation whose numbers are as the stars of heaven or the sand upon the seashore. Blessing also means the possession of a covenant—both a command and a promise; it is everything that defeats the state of exile, promising a life within time that yet holds back time's depredations and chaotic violence. It furthermore includes a principle of reciprocity: "Cursed be he that curseth thee, and blessed be he that blesseth thee" (Genesis 27:29). For Jacob in particular, such blessing is not something to be taken for granted. It is something won through luck and guile, baffled patience and aggressive righteousness. In securing Jacob's blessing from the aging Isaac, Jacob's "wise mother" was herself ready to use cunning, disguise, and falsehood, to risk a curse. Luther writes that he is astonished by Rebekah's courageous lie. Like Calvin and other commentators, he sees a mixture of human trickery and sacred theft, a story that witnesses both sinful evil and the power of faith. We should note that the sheep trick—"an act of shrewdness and almost of villainy" (Luther)—has an element of both economic calculation and revenge (along with a bit of natural magic); it's not only a way of getting back stolen wages, but also turns the tables on Laban for that bed trick by which Jacob found himself married to Leah instead of Rachel, for whom he was obliged to work another seven years. Laban is a type of usurious greed in some contemporary commentary, as Joan Ozark Holmer writes, and Shylock the usurer is more like him than he'll admit; but Jacob is himself not pure of such calculation. Throughout *The Merchant of Venice*, Shylock's willed identification with Jacob is part of his power. Like Shylock, Jacob is something of a trickster and improviser, a profiteer and even a thief of divine blessing, taking advantage of hazard and fortune, which includes "the work of generation." He speaks for an economy of blessing unreadable in either strictly material or spiritual terms—Shylock's amazing idea of "woolly breeders" is one index of the difficulty of describing it. There are also many moments in Jacob's history when such blessing, such chosenness, is hardly to be distinguished from a curse, exposing him to danger as much as protecting him. For Jacob, blessing is something gained by wrestling with that mysterious visitor who comes to him at night at the ford of the Jabbok, just at the moment when he is about to cross back into Canaan; his opponent is a figure read variously as angel, god, ghost, and demonic double. From this wrestling match Jacob emerges wounded but renewed, renamed Israel. Shylock gains no new name in this play, becomes the father of no new people; rather, he loses his daughter, who steals from him the ring given to him by his own Leah, and he all but cuts himself off from the Jewish community and Jewish history. Yet he engages in his own kind of wrestling match, one that causes his given name to stick to him with shocking force, so that it becomes a thing with a life of its own; that name begets its own kind of literary and cultural progeny in other worlds.

Shylock can also improvise sharply on New Testament narratives, as when he refuses Bassanio's invitation to supper: "Yes, to smell pork, to eat of the habitation which your prophet the Nazarite conjured the devil into" (1.3.29–30). This makes the Jesus of the Gospel of Mark himself reinforce, with sly wit, the Jewish prohibition against eating pork (the one concrete piece of Jewish sacred law that Shakespeare seems obsessed with in this play). But Shylock's hidden affiliations are more frequently with the patriarchal history. In the scene where he threatens Antonio with a knife, he recalls the narrative which is called in Jewish tradition the *akedah*, the binding, where Abraham holds a knife to his child's throat in order to fulfill his covenant with God. This image of the patriarch as "sacred executioner" is something that the Christians in the play might take as a fearful symbol of the church's own vexed relation to Jewish tradition, the ground of their antagonism to that tradition—though in Shakespeare's play the threat is made to show forth more human if no less stunningly opaque motivations. If Shylock mirrors Jacob and Abraham, his relation to Jessica can put us in mind of Isaac, likewise a father tricked by his own child out of bestowing his blessing as he might wish. This story is echoed more explicitly, and with bitter comedy, in act 2, scene 2, where Shylock's servant, the clown Lancelot, tricks his "sand-blind" father, old Gobbo, into thinking his son is dead. The scene in fact gives us a palimpsest in which the young Jacob's gulling of Isaac overlays memories of old Jacob himself tricked (as if in revenge) by his own sons, who show him the bloody coat of Joseph as proof that the boy has been killed by a wild beast. Lancelot, as if he is embarrassed to sustain the deception, eventually kneels down before old Gobbo to accept his blessing, but not before the clown-father seizes the occasion himself to deny that the mocker at his feet can be his son at all. It is this sort of scene that should give us a sense of how the texture of biblical allusion works in the play. The Bible narratives are part of the vernacular of the world, haunting in their way, also things to be played with, dramatic and rhetorical tools. The allusions point to some more ancient story subtending the conduct of life in a modern city, thick with circumstance. The effect is to create a picture whose spiritual and psychological implications are not at all clear.

The radical playfulness of Shakespeare's Old Testament allusions is what helps to set him apart from contemporary interest, especially among Protestant reformers, in biblical history and its textual particulars, a concern that spurred the revival of the study of Hebrew in Europe, including England, throughout the sixteenth century, along with a more intense study of the tradition of rabbinic commentary. Christian fascination with Jewish sources had many faces. It could be driven by a missionary zeal to convert the Jews, or a desire better to decipher the urgent historical warnings of apocalyptic texts like the book of Daniel. These studies also fed on the conviction of some humanist scholars, such as the controversial Johannes Reuchlin and Pico della Mirandola, that truths about the Trinity and the Incarnation could be discovered in the five books of Moses through the textual manipulations and numerological techniques of Jewish Kabbalah—this tradition in turn helping to suggest hidden but essential ties between Jewish scripture and other ancient sources of wisdom, such as Pythagoreanism, Platonism, and Hermetic magic. Such investigations often led Christian Hebraists, both Catholic and Protestant, to be branded as heretical "juda-izers." The crucial thing, however, is that a closer study of the language of the Hebrew Bible reflected the critical impulse of re-formers, the desire to cut through a tradition of error, to find a pristine ground of ancient truth by which to challenge the inherited medieval readings of the Old Testament as the well as the church doctrines, laws, and ceremonial institutions they supported, read-ings most often grounded in the Latin Vulgate translation of Saint Jerome. This project also contributed to the work of translating the Old Testament into the vernacular, or even into more accu-rate Latin versions, so as to give Christian readers a sharper, less mediated access to the divine and literal text. If Protestant com-mentators were bound to discover in Jewish scripture lessons that mirrored their own concerns with the workings of election and grace, the nature of blessing and reprobation, the nature of provi-dence, and the responsibility of preachers, their readings of the Old Testament yet understood the careers of the patriarchs as more than merely empty typological symbols or shadows of a fuller, fu-ture revelation. As James Samuel Preus makes clear, these biblical characters started to be taken up by reformers as particularized images of a spiritual life that fallen human beings live in the pres-ent. William Tyndale, in the prologue to his 1530 translation of the Pentateuch, speaks of the power of the homely "plain text and literal sense," never once mentioning typology, save to condemn those "great clerks" who say that "they wot not what more profit is in many gests of the scripture if they be read without an alle-gory, than in a tale of Robin Hood." The patriarchal history, even in representing a nation under Law, offered Protesant readers stark images of the sinful conscience's struggle with a covenant whose scope is not entirely known and with a God who is remote and vengeful; it showed images of a religious world threatened always by idolatry and stories of a sacred nation in exile, at odds with both God and itself. Luther's Genesis commentary, for instance, retells the Jacob and Esau story with a novelist's attention to situational complexities and psychological conflicts, even as he explains its relevance to the spiritual struggles of contemporary Christians.

Shakespeare is unlikely to have known any Hebrew, though he might have heard points of translation debated in contemporary sermons; nor would he have known rabbinic commentaries, however midrashic his comments on Jacob's sheep trick may sound. Throughout his plays, however, he shares something of this Protestant interest in evoking the dramatic force of Old Testament narrative, its "candid realism . . . which acknowledges a people's creatureliness and imperfection" and thus acts a remedy for the violence of a spiritualizing hermeneutics. We can see this, for example, in the ways that Macbeth mirrors the self-destructive career of Saul, that king who consults a witch to call up ghosts to tell him what he already knows about his loss of power and blessing. We see it in King Lear's complex doubling of the cursing and desolate Job. We see it in Othello's allusive ties to Moses, the alienated and wandering savior of his adopted nation; the moor dies (as Tom Bishop suggests) recounting a story that recalls the youthful Moses's murder of an Egyptian who beat a Hebrew slave. Yet in these and other cases, the biblical connections are deployed in ways that are simply too free, ambiguous, and fragmentary to allow them to serve the ends of doctrinal or typological coherence. There is little in Shakespeare's Old Testament echoes that suggests any interest in a critical philology or a polemical return to ancient sources of truth. If anything, the poet reminds us of a contingent strangeness and literary playfulness vitally present in the original narrative sources themselves.

Shakespeare's allusive freedom is evident in *The Merchant of Venice*'s most startling use of a biblical mirror. If at many moments in the play Shylock doubles the human participants in the patriarchal history, Abraham, Isaac, and Jacob, he also doubles the patriarch's god, Yahweh, a deity who is protean, capricious, resentful, and secretive, a god whose essence lies exactly in his unpredictability. Yahweh is a supernatural agent who inhabits the changing domain of time, shamelessly able to change his mind, to take advantage of a sudden occasion. Yahweh makes stern tests of human purity, dallies with human sacrifice, even murder, and mingles blessing and mercy with rigor and revenge in a way the Pauline dialectic cannot compass. He is a creator of contingent fates even as he is a creator of the world and animator of dead matter. This is not to say that the Yahweh of Genesis is a god such as Shylock might imagine for himself, much less one he would worship. Shylock never speaks about God, though he does speak of heaven. Rather, it is as if Shylock were Shakespeare's reimagining of the fate of this complex, ancient Jewish divinity in a human world, in human history. The poet reanimates and humanizes this god in a way that contributes to his reanimating and humanizing of the stereotype of the bloodthirsty Jew. In Shylock, that is, the play imagines the human motives, the human rage, vindictiveness, and guile that might drive such a god or bring him to birth. Shakespeare's invention implicitly reminds us that such gods are always human imaginings, forms of human life, even as, in Harold Bloom's terms, they make visible and put to the test the "theomorphic" aspects of the humans with whom they engage, the wrestler Jacob among them. Shylock is a vision of what happens to Yahweh in a Christian world that is also a strongly secular world, a god bound to the intractable pull of bodies, time, chance, fortune, politics, and human law. Following Theodor Reik, we might bring in the analogy of Heinrich Heine's essay "The Gods in Exile," which tells the story of how after the triumph of Christ the classical gods took refuge in the world of time, exiling themselves in homelier human forms. So Mars becomes a soldier, Mercury a Dutch merchant, and Bacchus a father superior in a monastery. In another poem of Heine's, Apollo the singer takes on the mask of a Jewish cantor, who in the end becomes a dissolute actor and clown. Thus degraded, these gods yet continue to speak for preternatural, unsanctioned, even demonic impulses that have been abandoned or neglected, set aside in the face of more idealistic pictures of divinity. In his mirroring of Yahweh, Shylock reinforces the play's larger refusal of the logic of Pauline theology, since the Hebrew god is so much larger in scope than any Pauline reduction of his being to a god of Law, let alone a vengeful tyrant (the Gnostic solution to the problem of the Old Testament god). At the same time, Shylock as Yahweh offers no alternative divinity to worship. There is no debt owed to this god that does not belong to a secular world, a world in which he finds himself made and remade. He is a god who is alien, rejected, but too close to home not to seem a threat.

Shylock as Yahweh is a creature god who offends, himself being offended, yet is also magisterial, capable of extravagant acts of generosity and cruelty. No less than Yahweh, he can be the avatar of a grim sort of clowning. I have suggested above how much Shylock is a clown in his way of taking up antisemitic stereotypes. Shylock is a clown in his biblicism as well, most powerfully in his mirroring of that deity whom Herbert Marks once compared, with inspired insight, to the figure of Punch, the assertive, noisy, improvisatory, hunchbacked, word-twisting, and devil-slaying puppet.

If Shakespeare himself, seen as a creator of forms of life, is any sort of god, he is most like Yahweh in the Book of Job. This god is like the playwright in his aim to astonish his auditor, facing Job with forms of life that combine the gorgeous and the terrible, facing him at the same time with questions about those creatures that have no answer, questions that should also make those who listen an astonishment to themselves. This god makes a pact with his mocking adversary cruelly to test Job's righteousness. He condemns those who attack the suffering, protesting Job for impiety or pride, who insist that he give up his rage and acknowledge his sinfulness, abasing himself before God's unknowable but certain justice. Yet Yahweh makes no direct answer to Job's cries for a divine accounting. If he blesses his rage, he meets Job's demand for an explanation by showing him something that defeats explanation, the wonder of the created world, a world whose creatures both reveal and hide Yahweh's powers, his difficult blessing. Speaking out of a whirlwind, Yahweh shows Job dancing stars and the mysteries of rain, but mostly a parade of beasts whose unpredictable vitality feels eerily human: the wild ass whose home is the desert; the ostrich so careless of its children; the stallion thrilled with its own force, laughing at the smell of war; the eagle seeking prey, whose young suck up blood; the huge and placid Behemoth; and lastly that vast water-dragon Leviathan, whom none can catch, whom none can make a covenant with, whose heart is as hard as a millstone, "King over all the children of pride." "Who shal open the dores of his face?" Ask that of Shylock, too, who has his own Job-like rages. Indeed, if Yahweh answers Job's human resentment with a sense of wonder, Shakespeare helps to remind us that such resentment, such rage and revolt, is itself a wonder, even a blessing—as Søren Kierkegaard thought, feeling himself blessed by the example of Job's protests to God.

That Shylock comes into the Venetian court so complexly caught up in recollections of Old Testament figures, human and divine, is one way in which the play dismantles any too simple a Pauline theater of Law and Mercy. Just as much is such a theater compromised by Portia, who is herself its chief architect and yet who makes one conscious of that theater's opportunism as much as its sacredness.

In the opposition of Shylock and Portia—whom here see each other for the first time—we witness a kind of localized war of the theaters. Portia disguised as a young lawyer speaks for a very different idea of dramatic power from what we see in the case of Shylock. The masks of Portia's theater do not hew so closely to the face as those of Shylock's. They do not burn into the skin. They give the wearer power, they allow her to explore otherwise unrevealed resources of mind, will, and language. But the donning of such a mask does not subject Portia to her own darkness, as Shylock's does, or provoke in others such a feeling of doubt and menace. Her theater rather shows us the actor as witty, pragmatic disguiser, someone concealed from others and yet not concealed from herself, perhaps because there is nothing to conceal. It makes her into a knowing allegorist, but never a daimonic agent. Her action is not without its mortal stakes and has a powerful, almost magical charm. Yet if Portia, shamanlike, presides over an exorcism, even a sacrifice, helping to remove a demon from the community, this is for her a bloodless ritual. It leaves her untouched and untransformed, having hazarded nothing.

Before Portia enters, Shylock has been holding up to Venetian law a mirror in which it may not want to see itself, a vision of its impotence, its complicity with an enemy of the state. A new and urgent charge falls on the stage as the young visitor arrives, dubbed with the name Balthazar—the name of one of the three Magi, also a version of Belteshazzar, the name given to Daniel in Babylon. Now the courtroom's hopes of a deus ex machina are focused, and claims for mercy get suddenly articulated. Dramatistically speaking, Portia enters as a kind of angelic visitant. Her entrance is a gift to the court, also to the audience, a relief from the bafflement that has attached itself to Shylock; she is also a more evolved, more stately double of Shylock's cross-dressed, baptized daughter Jessica (though Shylock is spared the knowledge of this). The famous first speech to Shylock opposes his rigid demand for law with the principle of heavenly mercy. She frames the issue as an eschatological one—asking him to acknowledge his own sinfulness and fear of judgment, somewhat as the comforters do to Job in the face of his stark demand for justice. But she quickly admits that this is an issue outside the law, something outside her command and only in the control of Shylock. Portia herself, in strictly legal terms, cannot compel his mercy, and indeed gives up the appeal to mercy when he ardently refuses it. In what follows, she turns herself into a legal ascetic, more dispassionately legalistic than Shylock himself. She acknowledges the clear justice of his claim with an alacrity that may surprise even Shylock (something intended to throw him off guard, no doubt). For a long interval, she holds off mentioning any specific legal means to get Antonio off the hook. Rather, taking the measure of the trial and its participants, she stretches out the nightmare of legal blame that Shylock has framed, seeming to sustain his vision of the law's awful precision and mercilessness. Antonio is her object here as much as Shylock; the merchant is made to feel just how much at risk he is (and, eventually, how much he will owe to Bassanio's wife). Overall Portia's arguments are neither trivial nor merely a cruel feint. She can seem cold blooded, but behind her talk of the law's mercilessness is a crucial dream of law as something that does not respect persons; it reflects a desire for an evenness or equity in law that cannot be bent by the arbitrary will of those in power, a wish for a law with a responsibility to its own history, its future as well as its past. Hence the danger, as Portia puts it, that in setting aside the law, for whatever reasons, the court would create a damaging precedent. In response to Shylock's demand that he be allowed the grim forfeit of his bond, she says, "the court awards it, and the law doth give it (4.1.296)." A few lines later, she repeats this ringing formula about the law's generosity with a chiastic inversion, "The law allows it, and the court awards it," inviting us to feel the force of the personification of the law, as well as to sense her own astonishing claim to speak for the court of Venice. By granting Shylock the right to take a pound of flesh from Antonio, she may seem strangely to rationalize his claims, or to drain them of their vicious mystery. That is to say, her words lend to Shylock's desires a kind of public candor, an inevitable fit within the world of law and its public articulation. Abetting Shylock's irrational violence, she also makes it seem clean and impersonal, embedded within a comprehensible legal ritual. This has the effect of silencing everyone onstage, committing us to a horrified wonder and anticipation. Portia is alone with Shylock in understanding how much the play can challenge its audience.

If her sudden skill seems surprising, we might recall that she brings with her to Venice not only the letters of Bellario but the lessons of Belmont, a place that has been to her both law school and dramatic academy. It has taught her about the double bind of legal contracts and legacies, and about how choices supposedly based on reason disguise vanity and unreason, also about how human choosers lend to the accidents of fortune the name of fate. She has learned there how to tempt those she dislikes into being caught by their own erring desires. In Belmont, her bondage to the casket ritual has taught her to play with stereotypes, to equivocate and speak against her own speaking, blankly to prevaricate, even to manipulate such binding rituals to her own ends. And she still bears with her into the heart of Venice the ambition of the Belmont world to contain what is explosive, dangerous, and unmeasurable.

When Shylock unsheathes his knife at the climax of the scene, its threat is at once concrete and hallucinatory. It is the switch point for everything that must be shown and yet hidden onstage— bodies, thoughts, passions, blood. This is the thing that will cut off the pound of flesh "nearest the merchant's heart," that will "cut off" the merchant himself from life. It is the intimate mark of Shylock's hatred, fixing his refusal of Christian mercy. We see in the knife the extruded form of that bond which he has made the center of his identity, the bond that possesses him, all that is left in place of stolen caskets and a faithless daughter. Memories of ritual sacrifice hover over the weapon; Shylock is Abraham preparing to kill Isaac, as I've suggested. At the same time, the knife remains an iconic tool of the bloodthirsty Jew of medieval folklore. (Is this the knife that can prick Jews, and make them bleed?) When Shylock carefully hones the knife on the leather of his boot, Gratiano, the perennial railer, cries, "Not on thy sole, but on thy soul, harsh Jew, / Thou mak'st thy knife keen. But no metal can, / No, not the hangman's axe, bear half the keenness / Of thy sharp envy" (4.1.123–26)—the crude pun pulling the physical knife further into the moral, psychological, and metaphysical drama of the scene. What is especially fascinating here is how much Portia herself makes the knife's dreamlike menace present with arcane, pseudomathematical precision, when in cadences at once charming and mocking she invites Shylock to cut off nothing but flesh without blood, and nothing more than a pound of flesh. The menace is there even though she describes a revenge we know is lost, made impossible, a revenge that for Shylock himself had been a wild gamble and that had promised a triumph which remained barely intelligible. Again, she pulls into play Shylock's rage, gives it form, even as she empties it out, thwarts it. She acts as a rabbi overseeing her own ironic version of the laws of *kashrut*. "This bond doth give thee here no jot of blood," she says, recalling the language of Christ about the authority of the Law in secular time: "For truely I say unto you, Til heaven, and earth perish, one iote, or one title of the Law shal not scape, til all things be fulfilled" (Matthew 5:18). She also echoes the revised covenant given to Noah after the flood, when Yahweh leaves men free to eat the flesh of animals but *not* the blood—in part, it seems, because blood appertains to sacrifice and to a divine economy of atonement for sin, of which murder is the cardinal instance: "Everie thing that moveth & liveth, shal be meat for you: as ye grene herbe, have I given you all things. But flesh with the life thereof, I meane, with the blood thereof, shal ye not eat. For surely I wil require your blood, wherein your lives are. . . . Whoso shedeth mans blood, by man shal his blood be shed: for in the image of God hathe he made man" (Genesis 9:3–6).

Portia, in appealing to an earlier covenant, may seem to be more Jewish than Shylock, trumping new law with old law. Lisa Freinkel writes that "like the laws of Moses, bewildering (as Luther tells us) in their number and complexity, the Law proliferates wildly in Portia's hands, branching out in every direction, its reach ever more extensive, its satisfaction ever more patently impossible—and it does so in order to compel that which cannot be compelled." So Portia says to Shylock, "Thou shalt have justice more than thou desirest" (4.1.312). It is exactly this fantastic, cunning deployment of law, as well as its way of being used for dramatic effect, as torture and temptation, that must strike us. Many scholars have taken Portia's plot to kill the bond as mirroring the exercise of legal equity, an ancient principle in legal theory that was described by Renaissance jurists as the conscience or mercy of law, its secret "sowle and spyrit." The discipline of equity asked judges to probe the intentions of the original lawgivers as well as the particular circumstances of alleged crimes, and so hopefully secure true justice in cases in which the letter of the law, followed rigidly, would lead to injustice. Yet one might also see in Portia's actions not a redemptive principle of equity, but rather an image of the law being used to sustain a terrible lawlessness or "anomy," as Theodore Ziolkowski has argued. However much bound to legal technicalities, her actions would thus reflect "a situation where norms have disappeared, where behavior has become unpredictable, where the law itself has become questionable"—the law's main importance to Portia being as a tool for a precise sort of dramatic improvisation set against Shylock.

The insinuating quality of Portia's words is clearest in her "tarry," her "soft, no haste . . . ," as if she would master time as well as Shylock. When he is about to stalk out of court, thinking himself free, if without revenge or return on his loan, she turns on him one more time:

> Tarry, Jew:
> The law hath yet another hold on you.
> It is enacted in the laws of Venice,
> If it be proved against an alien
> That by direct or indirect attempts
> He seek the life of any citizen,
> The party 'gainst the which he doth contrive
> Shall seize one half his goods, the other half
> Comes to the privy coffer of the state,
> And the offender's life lies in the mercy
> Of the Duke only, 'gainst all other voice.

In which predicament I say thou stand'st;
For it appears by manifest proceeding
That indirectly, and directly too,
Thou has contrived against the very life
Of the defendant, and thou hast incurred
The danger formerly by me rehearsed.
Down, therefore, and beg mercy of the Duke. (4.1.342–59)

Her use of the legal category of attempted murder reduces all the mystery of Shylock's malice, his menacing opacity. Especially given our bafflement about what life or death Shylock has been seeking, the means he has employed, such a conclusion may be eerily disappointing, if inevitable. In her accusing Shylock of intending to kill a Venetian we suddenly hear not the brilliantly ironic embrace of literality that had saved Antonio from the terms of his careless bond, but rather the truth of the laws of Venice speaking against the truth of the Jew's hatred. The very word "alien" has an odd ring to it, despite its accuracy as a legal term for the status of Jews in Venice. It has never been used before in the play. We have heard Shylock called dog, cur, swine, usurer, devil, Jew, enemy, and inhuman wretch, yet he has felt like an inescapable denizen of Venice, a creature of the place, haunting street and market-place, known on the Rialto, owning his house and attending his synagogue. We should recall here that the play itself knows nothing about the Venetian ghetto; we get no sense of a legally separate region of Venice where Shylock must dwell. Perhaps the word "alien" ironically reflects something about the substance of his danger, the reason for his being hated by the community that makes use of him, for within the social and economic orders of Venice Shylock is not an alien at all. The scene shows us the Venetians' revenge against a creature who may remind them too much of themselves, of their own bondage to law and money, to the making of infectious profit, not to mention slavery. The figure of the hated Jew has been a creature onto whom they can project and make alien their guilt, including their unacknowledged guilt over persecuting Jews. The word "alien" also serves Portia here insofar as it strips Shylock of the more resonant, arcanely mythic terms of abuse that he had made his own, made his mask and the feeder of his rage, and that he had used to shame the Venetians in turn. The word tries to contain an otherness more absolute, harder to find a name for. This is a preparation for making him vanish more completely from the scene.

The end of act 4 fails to provide any dramatic vehicle for the tragic wound that one feels in Shylock; the play, the theater of Portia, cannot bear to acknowledge it, or does not know how to. Everything made present by Shylock's rages is driven underground. Everything is put back into boxes, into caskets, resolved in conformity with outward rules, legalized gestures of mercy, generosity, and spiritual change. To the extent that Shylock represents something of a discovery for Shakespeare, an opening up of a kind of character that will become the fuel of his later plays, we may even sense a loss of nerve in the playwright, a failure of the will to hazard all he has or to carry out his invention to the letter. One could say that he has not yet found the right means to sustain such rage as Shylock's, the right contract or covenant with his own language and with the audience; he has not yet found a way to measure the dramatic costs of that rage, to draw stranger profits from it, to make it a currency within a larger structure of theater. Shylock cannot spend his rage and sorrow in a larger world within this play. They collapse on themselves.

The muteness of Shylock at the close is telling. In Jonathan Miller's production for the National Theatre (televised in 1973), Laurence Olivier's Shylock left the council chamber with a strangled "content." It was only from offstage, as the Venetians stood in a kind of baffled, even shameful silence, that their victim let loose a truly frightening sound. It began as an angry howl that moved into an intense fit of sobbing, sobbing that then slid into a high-pitched, barely human "eeeeeee" before fading away. That offstage noise drew one more shockingly toward the idea of Shylock's suffering and perhaps his eventual death. Stunning as this was, it may remind us the more forcefully of the lack of a tragic matrix or surround in the text of the play itself. The absence of any final vehicle for Shylock's rage makes it harder to measure or mourn Shylock's defeat, or to build a sense of a future on that loss. The one thing we are left to pursue is the idea of Shylock's conversion, something that acknowledges and turns against itself the troubling, occluded interior life we have seen in Shylock.

Shylock is forced offstage by the trial that he himself called forth. He leaves the platform, says almost nothing, the play goes on and ends without him, in another place, a place he's neither visited nor even heard of. He knows how to get offstage—what is an actor but a creature with a genius for entrances and exits?—but it is hard this time, so much energy is expended without a clear catastrophe. He remains standing in the wings, frozen in place, his face drained of blood, looking at the play or looking at nothing. Always the silence after the noise, or the noise that silences speech. It is the same for me. I must remove myself from the play that I have made, I am pushed off stage by that play, tricked by my own design out of whatever wishes for revenge or justice I'd wanted to make real, whatever sermons I'd wanted to preach. This, I have learned, is the law of the play, that the work in the end casts me out, drives me away, or takes itself off elsewhere as I stand rigid in collapsing space. There is no appeal, nor any life or living for me, save through that shameful, necessary bondage to a law that enriches and strips me. You cannot call it a death—there is no real death here, it is a rule of comedy that no one can die on stage. The truth of my play's last act is in Shylock's absence from it, and that is something, or enough, like a death. It mirrors my own needful absence from the play I've made possible, the play whose god I am in a world where other gods have exploded themselves, master of the shadows which I make part of a real world, bigger and more undying than my own, but yet moves as I myself am moved, in the mock court of an endless sterile reign of truckle and mow.

I leave an endowment to those who remain on stage when Shylock is driven off. The legacy is not gold or property, but something that sticks in the words that Lorenzo and Jessica use in Belmont. It's in the way they speak and the way they hear. These new skills of tongue and ear come through in their talk of the silence of the night, talk of moonlight sleeping on the bank, the spell of music, the image of the sky "thick inlaid with patens of bright gold," and in their sudden reach into a hidden world, the realm of the unseen angels whose music guides each star, unheard by mortal ears. The gift lies in their acknowledging darker things, the dress of the body's decay, the possibility of love's loss, thoughts about fear, humiliation, murder, and rage, stratagems and spoils, the lion's shadow. "The man that hath no music in himself" lacks it now because he has given it to others. Listen to what breaks through, ironically bestowed, waiting, rehearsing, with a smothered laugh, lurking in the comfort of light, even moonlight, darkness and fire at once. Can you imagine Shylock by moonlight? Or a Shylock hidden in the shadows cast by moonlight? You are looking at me.

Chapter Ten

CONVERSION

Defeated by Portia's law tricks and subject to the judgment of the Venetian court, Shylock is told that he must on pain of death become a Christian. Even if one feels strongly the hovering claims of mercy in this scene, feels the wish for some force that could break or soften the rigid claims of law, the idea of Shylock's conversion jars. It is Antonio and not Portia who proposes the conversion; he comes up with the idea suddenly, unpredictably, in the aftermath of his own unexpected salvation, as a codicil to two other proposals, coolly mean in themselves: "I am content," he says, "to quit the fine for one half of his goods," which the court had awarded him, provided that Shylock give half his money to Antonio "in use" for Lorenzo and Jessica and that he sign a will leaving his fortune to them in a posthumous deed of gift. The demand that Shylock convert is confirmed by the Duke of Venice, who makes it a condition of his continuing to hold out the earlier preemptive display of clemency ("That thou shalt see the difference of our spirit, / I pardon thee thy life before thou ask it" [4.1.364–65]). The proposal is cruelly gratuitous, at best a parody of free grace, mercy, or blessing, a mockery of any generous acceptance of an alien soul within a Christian community; it cannot without strain be taken for "part

106

of the process of internalizing justice" that Northrop Frye sees as proper to the end of a comedy. The demand that Shylock become a Christian hasn't even the blind arrogance of a spiritual or political order which, in totalitarian fashion, knows that it knows the needs of its members better than they themselves do. No one onstage can think that conversion would penetrate so violent a heart, much less advance the millennium, a fantasy at work in much Tudor writing about the conversion of the Jews, as James Shapiro has shown. The demand for conversion rather has in it the inventiveness of a cynical malice. It is the last twist of the knife in the staged humiliation of this Jew, one that tries to outmatch the Jew's humiliation of the merchant. By just so obviously not having any inward force, the idea of conversion reminds us of the more intractable spaces of mind and imagination the play has opened up in Shylock, even as it seems like an attempt to shut them down, or simply make them irrelevant.

The playwright himself added the forced conversion to the old story of the pound-of-flesh bond, derived from such sources as Giovanni Fiorentino's collection of comic tales, *Il Pecorone* (The simpleton), written in the fourteenth century and published in Milan in 1558. This adds to one's sense of its contingent perversity. In Fiorentino's version of the tale, for example, there is no conversion; the nameless Jewish moneylender merely tears his bond and retreats in a rage. The addition that Shakespeare makes is so blunt that it is hard to know its weight or to find the right language to speak about it. Shylock's blank, almost mute acceptance of the terms offered to him itself seems to reflect this. "I am content," he says, echoing Antonio's "I am content" just moments before, as well as the merchant's earlier acceptance of the bond in act 1: "Content, in faith, I'll seal to such a bond." Shylock's few words after "I am content" are "I am not well. Send the deed after me / And I will sign it" (4.1.392–93). It is as if there were nothing more for him to say; he has no resources left, and any illusion that the legal system might abet his will to revenge has collapsed on itself.

There are many ways we might imagine the actor uttering that last "content"—in a voice that is low, bitter, ironic, or mad. The main thing is that the dramatic text is so stripped and the surrounding silence so hard to frame. We have this description of the mute, inward triumph of Henry Irving's Shylock, as he turned on Gratiano after his parting bit of raillery: "Slowly and steadily the Jew scanned his tormentor from head to foot, his eyes resting on the Italian's face with concentrated scorn. The proud rejection of insult and injustice lit up his face for a moment." That sounds compelling, but as with Olivier's howl it is a gesture that must supplement a text that leaves the actor very few cues. And yet even if Shylock were given a more resonant parting shot—such as Iago's "Demand me nothing; what you know, you know," or Timon's "Lips, let four words go by and language end," or Parolles's "Simply the thing I am shall make me live"—his words might have found no purchase. No one onstage seems interested in listening to him at all.

Shylock abruptly leaves the court; the Christian world wants to know no more about him, but it is not likely he will go out of our minds. Partly because he is denied a part in a completed action, he hovers in a kind of limbo. Shylock's menace was extreme. It opened up a conceptual and emotional space that the other characters could not compass or acknowledge. His absent presence is the more striking because of the doubling of his exile and his promised conversion, and because of the long scene that unfolds after his departure from the stage. During this time he is referred to only once, and then merely as "the rich Jew." The last act, with its moving evocation of cosmic music and its touching game of rings, offers us a sense of time restored, of fortune made right, of a happiness, a "life and living," that extend toward an unknown future. It attempts to banish the threat of Shylock. Yet even if one takes the scene in good faith, it is hard to keep Shylock from haunting one's consciousness. For one thing, everything we witness in Belmont is contingent on the trial that led to Shylock's defeat: the freedom of Antonio, the gift of money to Jessica and Lorenzo, and the very disguises of

Portia and Nerissa that make possible the climactic ring trick. Of course, one doesn't really want to hear what Portia and her friends would say about Shylock in Belmont, though perhaps it would be no more chilling than their silence.

The silence provokes questions, opens up troubling spaces of surmise. How do we imagine Shylock's fate after his departure from the stage? Can we imagine the scene of his baptism? Who would have stood as his godparents? What Christian name would he have taken? (Jacopo? Guglielmo?) What would the congregation have said or thought? Imagine his first Communion, his putting into his mouth the body and blood of Christ. Imagine his life in Venice after his baptism. Can one envision him conducting business among other Christian merchants at the Rialto, now free of the legal restrictions that forced Jews into moneylending? Or living contentedly with other neophytes in the Pia Casa dei Catecumeni, a residence set up by the Church in Venice for converted Jews, where they received instruction in their new faith? Or going regularly to Mass, where he might encounter Lorenzo and Jessica, or his old mocker Gratiano? Can we imagine him as madman or beggar walking the streets of Venice? (What curses or jests would he mutter to himself?) Or would he flee from Venice, either to wander alone or to join communities of practicing Jews in other nations, as many forced converts did? The fact that the Shylock who loomed so hugely now disappears makes it feel all the more necessary to face the absence.

There is a strange refinement of cruelty in Antonio's proposal. Strikingly, the cruelty entails an enlargement in our sense of Shylock's conflicted interiority and isolation. This becomes clearer if we call to mind the labyrinth of fear, doubt, despair, ambition, and guilt that shaped the experience of actual Jews forced to undergo conversion in late medieval and Renaissance Europe, especially Spain and Portugal, those who became what were called conversos, or New Christians. Of course, while some pieces of this history crept into the awareness of the Elizabethans—there were travelers'

CHAPTER TEN

tales and diplomatic reports, and John Foxe could write, in his anti-Catholic *Actes and Monuments*, of how "the cruell and barbarous Inquisition of Spayne" was "instituted agaynst the Jewes," who "after their Baptisme mainteined agayne their own ceremonies" and even describe how, in 1190, the Jews of York committed suicide to escape the choice between massacre or forced conversion—Shakespeare himself probably knew little about the struggles of converted Jews. But no one would have been more capable of imagining them.

This history is a complex one, casting a long shadow, and is still much debated by scholars. Some things are clear enough. During the Middle Ages, Jews were tolerated as witnesses to the triumph of the church, even as the hope of their conversion fed eschatological expectations. Conversion by force ran against official church rules. Canon law and papal proclamations since the time of Gregory the Great (590–604) spoke of the necessity of persuasion and the need to guard the consciences of potential converts from coercion, often denouncing violence and false accusation against Jewish populations. Yet from the earliest days of the church's consolidation under the authority of Rome, the conversion of Jews through the threat of death, imprisonment, expulsion, or loss of property, was a terribly common thing—and baptism, even if brought about by illicit means, was generally regarded as a sacrament that could not be annulled. Antonio's plan involves a blunter, more intensely localized display of legal revenge than any other instance I have read of. But it shadows in miniature the experience of Jews in Spain in 1391, for example, when vast numbers accepted baptism in the wake of anti-Jewish riots and massacres of Jewish communities that began in cities in Castile and spread to Aragon and Catalonia, stirred up particularly by the popular preaching of a friar named Ferrant Martínez. Two decades later, at the Tortosa disputation (1413–14), Jewish religious leaders from across Spain were compelled by the anti-Pope Benedict XIII to enter into public debate with Christian theologians over the truth of the Messiah and the authority of Jewish law—the church's chief spokesman being himself a converted Jew. In the shadow of this very controlled debate and its calculated humiliations, further mass conversions of Jews occurred, often publicly staged as examples to the rest of the Jewish populace. Under such conditions, "distinctions between conversion by persuasion and conversion by duress could not easily be drawn." Among those not ready to seek martyrdom or exile, conversion was something variously dictated, in Léon Poliakov's words, "by ambition or despair, by prudence or cowardice." Nor was conversion itself an end to their dilemmas. In Spain, Portugal, and Italy, Jewish converts to Christianity inhabited a deeply divided situation, their purported liberty marred by continued prejudice, suspicion, and legal restriction, their inner lives caught by doubt and the fear of violence. Conversos often remained an uncertain entity within Christian communities, whose antisemitic traditions remained intact and were even revivified by their presence; they had joined themselves to a faith in whose sacred texts and public sermons the Jew still figured as an alien, demonic enemy, or at best a rejected ancestor. This produced in the culture "a secret war where no holds were barred, in the name of a faith that was degraded by both sides equally." Sectarian hatred easily passed into racial hatred. An anonymous Spanish book from 1488 describes the New Christian as an apocalyptic monster with "a wolf's mouth, human eyes, the ears of a greyhound, the body of an ox, the tail of a snake and legs with the hooves of different animals." Communities of conversos suffered massacres as had communities of Jews, as in Lisbon in 1506, when two thousand New Christians were slaughtered by mobs. Especially in Spain and Portugal, statutes requiring "purity of blood" restricted Jews from intermarrying with Old Christian families and from joining certain guilds, colleges, and monastic or chivalric orders. Conversos were often prevented from emigrating, denied passports, lest they find their way to countries where they could shed their Christian identity and return to Judaism. They were surrounded by spies and accusers, even within their own households, ready to denounce them to the Inquisition for secret religious practice. Despite often meticulous and extravagant rules for distinguishing the true Christian, rage against conversos seems to have been focused precisely on the difficulty of distinguishing them from still-practicing Jews, or even of defining a Jew precisely. "If any distinction at all was made, it was to the advantage of the traditional Jew. After all, he was a familiar sight; he had been part of the Spanish scene since ancient times. The *converso* was too disturbing and too exasperating; he was the one the people tended to blame for everything that went wrong." Conversos might be equally at odds with the Jewish communities they had left (assuming that the community had not entirely been destroyed). If some Jews sought to draw converts back into the old religious ways, for others the converts became objects of distrust and hatred. Converts might be called in Hebrew, sympathetically, *anusim*, the forced ones. But they might also be condemned by rabbinic authorities as faithless apostates, *meshumadim*, literally, the destroyed ones, persons blotted out from the book of life. Such conversos might fall out of affiliation with Jewish history entirely.

The expulsion of Jews from Spain in 1492 aimed at purging their contaminating influence on the Christian kingdom, especially among conversos. The Spanish Inquisition, established in 1578, still continued relentlessly to seek out Jewish thought, practice, and blood, spiritual infection and political conspiracy, among the many conversos who remained.

Many conversos rose to positions of power at European courts, often trading on administrative skills and financial and personal networks that had been long developed among Jewish bankers and merchants. They might take the place of the court Jews that had previously been protected by European royalty. One scholar cites a fifteenth-century Spanish pamphlet that "mockingly advised Old Christians to become *conversos* so that they might reach the higher echelons of officialdom and business leadership." Others rose within the hierarchy of the church, including important religious thinkers such as Saint Teresa of Avila and Saint John of the Cross. Yet the process of absorption was scarcely without conflict. In the work of some converso authors, it has been argued, one finds a skeptical and agonized strain, the sense of "an exposed and solitary consciousness," that reflects their experience of being so constantly under suspicion, marked as alien or dangerous, and aware always of a mortal threat hovering in the background. Scholars have sensed this converso note—to mention just two examples—in the fierce critique of scholastic logic, pleas for religious toleration, and sense of moral crisis that mark the writings of the humanist pedagogue Juan Luis Vives; and in the anarchic intelligence of Fernando de Rojas, whose novel *La Celestina* (1499) depicts a world of deception driven by both passion and cynicism, always haunted by fears of betrayal, loss, shame, and arbitrary violence. Both authors came from converso families and knew themselves under suspicion by the "furtive, sacred, and despotic" machinery of the Inquisition. (Rojas's father was condemned to death by the Inquisition for judaizing and his father-in-law imprisoned for life for heretical utterances; Vives's parents were both condemned for secret Jewish practice, his father burned and his dead mother's bones unburied and burned.) It is clear that the widespread and often unpredictable persecution of Christians with Jewish backgrounds, and the fact that this was sustained by the very church that sought conversion of Jews, could leave converts deeply divided. Many of those who were baptized clearly became devout members of the Christian community (as Vives, for example, felt himself to be). For others, the experience of conversion ironically drew them into religious skepticism and heterodoxy. They might vacillate between the new and old religions, often inventing curious hybrids of both, or be caught by an inherent distrust of all religions, witnessing as they did their coerciveness, their hatred, hypocrisy, and liability to being practiced in disguise. The ranks of those professing Christianity included Jews who underwent repeated baptisms in different cities in order to secure the charity converted Jews received, and, in some cases, the licenses giving them the status of legal beggars or permitting them, like Chaucer's Pardoner, to work as itinerant vendors of rosaries, indulgences, and relics. The grimmest cases were those in which Jewish converts turned into the most zealous persecutors of Jews. These ranged from the crowd of petty informers used by the Inquisition to secure accusations against judaizers to intellectuals, politicians, and clerics who wrote treatises and sermons denouncing their former coreligionists, who helped shape the anti-Jewish laws, and even composed guides to help inquisitors better identify telltale Jewish practices among the newly baptized. The ruthless Tomás de Torquemada, first inquisitor-general of Spain, came from a converso family.

It will not be at all reassuring if we imagine Shylock, after his baptism, becoming one of that group of conversos who continued to practice in secret, the crypto-Jews or marranos (this label deriving, it is generally thought, from an old Spanish word for swine, itself derived from the Arabic *muḥarram*, "forbidden"). How many marranos there were in Europe, how they practiced their Judaism, how long marrano communities survived, whether their widespread existence was not, indeed, chiefly a paranoid and opportunistic fabrication of the Inquisition itself, are questions yet debated among historians. What has been said of them can only be sketched out here. Cut off from living contact with traditional Jewish life and religion, marranos were bound to the contaminations of a double life. They were always in danger of being found out, of being impeached by neighbors and even their own children (who typically were informed of their Jewishness only when they reached adolescence). To manifest any outward signs of their faith became a point of purchase for suspicion, especially in places emptied of openly practicing Jews. Duplicity and dissimulation were built into the warp and weft of things. If marranism was an outward danger, it was also an inner exile, if not an inner martyrdom. Such secrecy as it required might revive faith or provoke doubt. What records we have—many preserved only in the archives of the persecutors—suggest that secret Jews were bound to a world of shadowy, equivocal religious practices which had lost much of their connection with the actual rites and legal forms of rabbinic Judaism. The traditional rites that survived were often reduced and schematized, strongly influenced by the forms of Christian piety that converted Jews were compelled to study, or shaped by reference to Old Testament texts (read in Latin or Spanish) rather than Talmudic law. One signature form of marrano piety, for instance, was the belief that personal salvation lay in the Law of Moses. Marranos also worshipped a "Saint Esther," the disguised Jewess turned savior of her people. At best, among marranos, as Yosef Kaplan writes, the "inner psychological identification with Jewish religious and national heritage was more important than observance of the commandments of Jewish law." So a marrano worshipper might say to himself, "I lit the Sabbath candles only in my heart." The possibility of buried aggression or doubt in such cases might be overwhelming.

What Cecil Roth called the "romance" of the marrano and Poliakov "the marrano epic" reflects a religious, social, and intellectual crisis. It speaks for both a catastrophic loss of continuity with tradition and an ironic, secret, sometimes blind mode of survival. Just for these reasons, the situation of conversos and marranos has become for some scholars an emblematic image of the dilemmas of Jewish modernity, indeed, of modernity in general. Marranism could entail an experiment in thought, interiority, disguise, and assimilation, a way of bearing conflicts of religious allegiance and political and philosophical doubt. Carl Gebhardt thus wrote of "the cleavages in the marrano conscience from which the modern conscience has sprung." The marrano is an "epitome of the human soul, but what an epitome!" says Poliakov. The idea of an identity so vexed, so suspended between Christian and Jew, may in turn tell us something about the continuing fascination of Shylock, his singular typicality, his revelation and mystery.

Yosef Hayim Yerushalmi sees an exemplary figure of the dualities of marrano experience in the person of Isaac Cardoso. Cardoso was born in a Portugese marrano family around 1603. Having trained in medicine at universities in Spain, he rose to the highest ranks of Spanish intellectual and civic life, famous as a physician, philosopher, and poet, even as he continued to practice his Judaism in secret. At the age of forty-three he fled to Italy, first to Venice and later to Verona, where he became an openly professing Jew and an important figure within the Sephardic Jewish community, many members of which were similarly exiles from Spain and Portugal. His last book, *Las excelencias de los Hebreos* (1679), is both a passionate encomium to traditional Jewish theology and Law and a systematic defense of Jews against the ancient catalog of antisemitic slanders. What is crucial for Yerushalmi in the career is not just the breach, the costly yet liberating move from secrecy to openness, but Cardoso's ambition to heal that breach, to write a Jewish book whose argument and language yet continue to be fed by his training as a Christian humanist, classicist, and scientist. (The unconventional shape of such a story, especially in its undoing of any ambition toward mere assimilation or worldly success, is implicit in the title of Yerushalmi's study of Cardoso, which evokes its own reversal: *From Spanish Court to Italian Ghetto*.) It is this effort to reconcile in his writings the competing strains of his experience that makes Cardoso, for Yerushalmi, one of the most telling precursors of the Jewish enlightenment, or Haskalah.

Another crucial figure here is Baruch Spinoza, a heretic among the Jews of Amsterdam and a Jew without religion among Christians. ("He was solemnly expelled from the community of Israel and declared unworthy henceforth to call himself a Jew. His Christian enemies were magnanimous enough to let him keep this name," wrote Heinrich Heine.) Certain patterns of marrano experience, as Yirmiyahu Yovel and Gabriel Albiac argue, touch him deeply. They are visible in Spinoza's double exile; in his caution, in his sense of being the object of suspicion, even persecution; in his ingrained habits of disguise and equivocation in writing; in his hatred of sectarian conflict; and in his attachment not to custom or law but to a purer, more inward metaphysical truth, to a secret of salvation that for all its rational ground echoes a religious or a prophetic mode of knowledge, even as it involves a refusal "to save human beings from their essential destiny as things among things." Spinoza's *Theologico-Political Treatise* (1670) takes as its central example the polity of ancient Israel, describing it as both perfect and perfectly cursed, its laws guaranteeing at once piety and rebellion; it is a polity whose divinity lies in its exemplifying an order also at work in history and nature and hence points toward the ground for a critique of all state religion. In translating aspects of marrano spirituality into something more secular and universal, Spinoza becomes, in Yovel's resonant phrase, a "marrano of reason." His Jewishness is an increasingly mysterious yet essential possession. Spinoza makes clear how the difficulty of dividing Jew and marrano becomes part of the inner and historical destiny of the Jews.

The experience of secret practice, persecution, and expulsion also fostered an attachment among some marranos to Lurianic Kabbalah. At the core of this movement was a myth of divine exile and of creation as catastrophe. Here God contracts or withdraws into himself to allow space for creation, a self-alienation within divine being itself; he prepares vessels to be filled with his light that break apart at its influx. The pieces of these vessels fall into the lower world, where they mix with the shattered fragments of a cosmic Adam, a divine man who himself fell at the very moment he was prepared to redeem creation. Such fragments of the divine, however, believers could lift up and restore (*tiqqun*) by their piety, a piety that here takes on a magical or mystical coloring. While this strain of Kabbalistic thought did not itself originate among the Jews of Iberia, but rather among Jewish scholars in Palestine, it offered marranos and other Diaspora Jews a way to read their inward and outward exile as part of a cosmic history. It gave them a means of framing their lives within an apparently failed tradition of promise and yet looking beyond that failure to a moment when the world of exile might be wholly abolished. For Gershom Scholem, it is the historical self-consciousness and spiritual vitality of this strongly heterodox reinvention of Jewish tradition that helps to account for the astonishing enthusiasm among the Jews of the Diaspora—"from Marakesh to Vilno, and from Thessaloniki to Hamburg"—for the claims of an eccentric visionary from Smyrna named Sabbatai Tsevi. Beginning in 1665, Tsevi began to announce himself, with the help of his prophetic apologist Nathan of Gaza, as a Kabbalistic messiah, bringing to a climax the historical process of *tiqqun*. The great crisis of the movement is, for Scholem, also the definitive sign of its radicalism, its power to transvalue Jewish tradition. In 1666, visiting Adrianopole, Tsevi converted to Islam under threat of execution by the Turkish sultan, whose crown Tsevi himself had declared he would take up. Yet the force of the messianic promise was strong enough that many believers refused to submit their inward persuasion to "the cruel verdict of history." Rather than rejecting Tsevi as a false messiah, they were caught by a countermyth in which the messiah's apostasy, his abject degradation, contamination, and spiritual exile, became the means by which salvation continued, though under scandalous disguise. Tsevi's conversion was interpreted as a knowing act of self-sacrifice, an embrace of the world of sin. "Good has to assume the form of evil," becoming a kind of spy. In this myth, writes Scholem, "the Messiah must go his lonely way into the kingdom of impurity and 'the other side' (*sitra ahra*) and dwell there in the realm of a 'strange god' whom he would yet refuse to worship." Such a vision was the more compelling as it mirrored the troubled and deeply paradoxical experience of the marranos themselves. By this logic, Tsevi indeed becomes a voluntary rather than a compelled marrano. "It is ordained that the King Messiah don the garments of a Marrano and so go unrecognized by his fellow Jews. In a word, it is ordained that he become a Marrano like me." So writes Abraham Cardoso, younger brother of Isaac, and one of the most important proponents of the Sabbatian doctrine after the apostasy. Scholem throughout his life was absorbed by the dialectical freedom, even the nihilism, of this movement, "the half-light of a faith pregnant with paradoxes," including the antinomian idea of redemption through sin. It spoke to a sense of anarchic possibility, even liberating blankness, within Judaism and Jewish consciousness, though he also saw in this movement how "genuine desires for a reconsecration of life mingled indiscriminately with all kinds of destructive and libidinal forces tossed up from the depths by an irrepressible ground swell that undulated wildly between the earthly and the divine"—as in the libertinism and blasphemy that characterized the teachings of the Sabbatian Jacob Frank.

Scholars such as Scholem, Yerushalmi, and Yovel put the case that it is the line of marranism—with its heterodox, ironic, and often tragic relation to Jewish tradition, its haunting sense of the double life, of the burdens and pleasures of secrecy, as well as its openness to more conflicted currents of religious interpretation—that points the way to Jewish modernity. The representatives of this modernity include Moses Mendelssohn and Heinrich Heine, as well as such crucial twentieth-century Jewish writers as Sigmund Freud, Franz Kafka, Walter Benjamin, and Scholem himself. Robert Alter speaks of these last three as "necessary angels," playing on Wallace Stevens's "necessary angel of earth," a secular imagining of the angelic in whose sight "we see the earth again." For Alter, these authors struggle to articulate a sense of tradition in the "no-man's-land" between the sacred and the profane, between revelation and nihilism. Their writings reflect an inheritance of disenchantment, a perception of the decay of experience and the loss of redemptive possibility, that yet cannot release them from their attachment to the revelatory power of scripture and the generative work of interpretation, even in cases (such as Benjamin's) in which "a focus on the iconography of tradition serves the purpose of defining more sharply the disasters of secular modernity." The idea of a Jewishness that sustains itself within such a conflicted tradition, that indeed takes the struggle with tradition as itself a sustaining power, helps us to understand some of the reasons that Shylock haunts later writers, both Jewish and Christian. If Shylock's articulate rage against antisemitic hatred remains crucial to his power for us, what also counts here is the questions set to resonate by the idea of his forced conversion, by all that it clarifies and leaves mysterious. These questions help to bring him within the gravitational pull of the paradoxical history of Jewish modernity; they suggest why the figure of Shylock has become at once a touchstone and a stumbling block for those who try to write about the modern history of the Jews. They help us understand the fascination of Shylock's isolation, the power of his often ironic mirroring of biblical figures, his heterodox interpretive bent, and his anxious, costly freedom of thought; they also clarify how the idea of Shylock's survival plays so complexly against our sense of his continued victimhood. To link Shylock with the history of conversos and crypto-Jews may be most compelling, indeed, because it reassures us so little about what it means to speak of Shylock as a Jew, gives us so little ability to specify the kind of Jewish victim he is. It troubles any wish to save Shylock for Jewish tradition. It reminds us of just how vexed the creation of spiritual continuities can be, and how this process may be bound to the creation of false saviors or shape suspect images of suffering and loss, salvation and recuperation. If this background helps give some historical shape to the question of Shylock's interiority, it may serve best because it shows us sharply just how much we do not and cannot know about that interiority. Even what we might call Shylock's Jewishness has become, by the end of the play, a psychotic possession, a private language; we can neither fix it according to historical ideas of Jewish experience nor stigmatize it according to Christian myths of Jewish legalism, guile, and murderousness. What it means to lose that Jewishness then, or to drive it underground, becomes all the harder to specify.

Among modern Jewish writers, Kafka has often come to mind as I have worked on Shylock. I think of that writer's pictures of minds trapped in paranoid, opaque, and yet still luminous tangles of legal interpretation. The play's grim and playful animal imagery calls up Kafka's own half-human beasts, his curious visitants,

secretive, sacral, histrionic, violent, and vulnerable—the shy, terrified, and terrifying animal in the synagogue; the lamb-kitten,
predator and prey, pet and chattel; the desperate, self-doubting
burrower; or Kafka's upstart crows, creatures who maintain that a
single crow (*kavka* in Czech) could destroy the heavens. ("Heaven
simply means: the impossibility of crows.") Kafka was a man whose
fate, as Walter Benjamin said, was always to stumble upon clowns.
He found them even within scripture, such as his Abraham, who
when called to sacrifice his son refuses out of fear that he will turn
into Don Quixote. Benjamin wrote to his friend Scholem, scholar of
catastrophe, by way of challenge, "I think the key to Kafka's work
is likely to fall into the hands of the person who *is able to extract the
comic aspects from Jewish theology.*" He might have been talking about
Shakespeare in his making of Shylock.

In *A Natural Perspective*, Frye remarks that Shylock is the chief
exception to his theory that, at the end of Shakespearean comedies,
the defeated forces opposing comedy "become states of mind rather
than individuals." To such a conversion, he acknowledges, Shylock
remains resistant. Shylock for Frye is like "the eternal questioning Satan who is still not quite silenced by the vindication of Job.
Part of us is at the wedding feast applauding the loud bassoon;
part of us is still out in the street hypnotized by some greybeard
loon and listening to a wild tale of guilt and loneliness and injustice and mysterious revenge. There seems no way of reconciling
these two things. Participation and detachment, sympathy and
ridicule, sociability and isolation, are inseparable in the complex
we call comedy, a complex that is begotten by the paradox of life
itself." (Samuel Taylor Coleridge's Ancient Mariner is also in play
in these lines, along with his ancestor, the Wandering Jew.) Frye
here acknowledges a weak place in his own mythology of genre, a
crisis that the machinery of romantic comedy fails to accommodate.
Shylock as *idiotes* is indeed a shadow throughout Frye's book, a perennial scandal. He marks, among other things, the unnaturalness
that emerges within the domain of the natural.

The archives of the Inquisition in Venice contain records of the case of a woman named Elena de' Freschi Olivi, accused of blasphemy in 1555, after two witnesses reported her yelling at the priest during Mass, at the moment of the Credo. She shouted that he lied "through his throat" when he said the words "incarnatus est de Spiritu Sancto ex Maria Virgine et homo factus est," calling the priest (or Christ) "the bastard son of a whore." After this she made the sign of figs with her fists. Madonna Elena was the aging mother of a prominent converso physician whose Christian name was Giovanni Battista de' Freschi Olivi. He had obtained a doctor's degree in theology from the University of Padua and became well known for his public denunciations of the Jews, joining the commission charged with gathering rabbinic books for burning in 1553, under papal injunction—the destruction of the Talmud being the most marked of Giovanni Battista's many attempts symbolically to sever himself from an infected origin. (He had once, after his conversion, disguised himself as a Jew [!] to steal his children from the ghetto; he also divorced his first wife when she refused herself to convert.) Elena, a widow, had followed her son into Christianity when he had left the ghetto. Yet many episodes in her subsequent life suggest a confusing mixture of marranism and madness. In court she defended her piety before the judges, giving evidence of her sincere devotion to Christ since her conversion, her going to confession and receiving Communion, and her giving of alms to the poor. Witnesses provided more contradictory reports. Some spoke of her devotion and consistent religious practice, others of instances of irregularity and impiety, fasts on Jewish holidays, her continued refusal to consume forbidden meats, and her habit of muttering prayers or imprecations in Hebrew. She would call Christianity a "maledetta fede" (cursed faith) from which she wished to escape back into Judaism, even to flee to Jerusalem. She had been heard to utter such paradoxes as "who is not a good Jew cannot be a good

Christian." Other witnesses reported her disputes with persons in the empty air and her shouted promises to bring the law down on her enemies. She would threaten violence to priests, judges, and other nameless adversaries—"Ve farò squartar, ve farò impicar, ve farò amazar" (I'll have you quartered, I'll have you hung, I'll have you killed). Christ she called "porcho, poltron, ladro" (pig, sluggard, thief), worthy of having his nose and ears cut. She often tore up costly clothes and threw the rags into the latrine, as she sometimes also did with pieces of meat. The son's defense of his mother against the criminal accusation of judaizing, his answer to the "slanders" of other witnesses, was that the evidence pointed rather to her unbalanced mind. Her lunacy was in fact, he insisted, an ancient malady, one that he attributed to both natural and supernatural causes, including an excess of melancholy humors and the influence of malicious spirits (a diagnosis he supported with many learned glosses from the Gospels, Aquinas, and the *Malleus Maleficarum*). And yet the son also insisted that her conversion to Christianity, undertaken during a lucid interval, remained sincere, rather than a calculated and criminal lie. One historian suggests that the moments of madness allowed Elena to speak the impossible contradictions of her position, private and public. Her madness freed her to speak her Jewishness, both as an ordinary faith and as a ground of resentment; it allowed her to challenge Christian pieties, even as her Jewishness remained, at best, the "bloodless phantasm of that tradition" of which her son had deprived her. The decision of the judges, confining her to the great hospital in Treviso, was, in the event, somewhat thwarted. The hospital being unwilling to take such a patient, the Holy Office ruled that she be confined for life in a bedroom of her son's house, out of sight and hearing of the household and of passersby.

Chapter Eleven

GOLEMS AND GHOSTS

An examination of two more fully developed fictions of Shylock's afterlife will help to clarify what is at stake when we reimagine such a creature. The crucial question remains what it means to keep faith with Shakespeare's fiction.

One of the most elaborate attempts to lend Shylock a life that continues beyond the confines of the play is the 1931 novel *The Last Days of Shylock*, written by Ludwig Lewisohn—a prolific but now mostly forgotten American novelist, scholar, and man of letters. The narrative begins at the moment the trial is over. We watch Shylock ferried back to his house in the ghetto, silent and brooding. As he sits up all night in his study, awaiting his compelled baptism the next morning, he rehearses his youth, memories of which fill up much of the first half of the book. His parents are all but invisible. He remembers being taunted by Christian children and called a Christ killer; bullies make him kiss the bleeding carcass of a pig in a butcher shop. He is old enough to recall vividly the forced relocation of Jews to the ghetto in 1516, and he reflects on the intensified religious and artistic life the community lived there. He thinks also of the fearful season of Easter, when the gates of the ghetto were locked and heavily guarded to protect the Jews inside from vengeful mobs fired by the blood libel. The public burning of Jewish books in 1553, commanded by the pope for their alleged slanders of Christ and Christians, also looms large in his memory, for this Shylock is a man learned in Talmudic law. We see his futile pleading with the Venetian Council of Twelve, as he tries to show that the accusations against Jewish books are false; we see him coming to realize that it was the merchant Antonio, a man who had pretended to a sympathetic interest in Jewish learning, who revealed to the Venetian police where so many hidden books were to be found. Along with the burning of books, Lewisohn's Shylock has witnessed in Ancona, in 1556, the burning of twenty-four converted Jews convicted by the Inquisition of secretly practicing their old faith; he recalls how his terror at the sight was mixed with exaltation, an unspoken fascination with Jewish martyrdom. In general, Lewisohn imagines a Shylock conscious of the fate of Jews in Europe after their expulsion from Spain and Portugal, the endless wandering and the threat of persecution and death, as well as the implacable element of hope and messianic longing, sometimes compromised. As young man, for example, Shylock witnesses the visit to Venice in 1524 of the remarkable charlatan David Reubeni, who arrived in the city claiming to be the brother of the king of a lost tribe of Jews in central Arabia, seeking support from the pope and the Christian kings of Europe in raising an army against the shared threat of the Ottoman Turks.

What Lewisohn's Shylock knows of actual Christians is uncertain. He registers at moments the mystery of their relentless hatred and the fragility of all attempts at sympathy, though we never see him rehearse in his mind the trial as it unfolds in Shakespeare. He does recall a moment when, watching ordinary Christians laugh at a clown in a false nose playing a Jew in a carnival show, he suddenly sheds his hate for them, realizing that "it was their foul and arrogant superstition that made beasts and murderers of these fair men and women." This is a spot of time that he never forgets yet rarely dwells upon, "guarding it rather like a jewel too precious for the daily sunlight of the sinful earth." It is a reminder of what the theater may reveal to us as well. This is, I should say, a rare allusion to the novel's source in a theatrical work, and to its complex treatment of masking. For just a moment, Lewisohn's Shylock sees what will become of him on the stage, even as he senses how the virulence of this image might be cured.

We learn in the novel that Shylock is a usurer not out of a miserly passion for gold or earthly power, much less because he wants to bankrupt Christians. The money gained rather serves the work of charity both in Venice and the larger world, aiding the poor, repairing synagogues, and paying burdensome taxes and fines, as well as ransoming Jews captured by pirates or sold into slavery, as rabbinic law requires. It is Shylock's integrity with money, as well as the scope of his international connections, that has led to his becoming the (covert) Venetian agent of the House of Mendes—a family of Portuguese conversos who created a banking house of huge influence throughout Europe. By the mid-sixteenth century, the family had its shifted base of operations from Lisbon and Antwerp to Venice, and then later, still under threat from the Inquisition, moved to Istanbul, where they could return to the open practice of Judaism. Here—and in this Lewisohn is being strictly historical—the head of the family, João Micas, took the name Joseph Nasi, becoming a powerful political adviser of the Turkish sultan, rewarded eventually with the title of duke of Naxos (making him sovereign over an island predominantly Christian). In the novel, it is Nasi who aids Shylock in his flight from Venice just after his baptism (an event which itself is all but occluded in the book, regarded cynically by Shylock and described only briefly between the long reminiscence of its first half and the continuing history of its second).

The scenes of the novel set in Venice have real imaginative force. They catch at the psychological and moral thickness of

Shakespeare's play, mining its spaces of uncertainty and question, even as they try to give them a certain historical specificity, to reframe them in relation to facts that Shakespeare would not have known. In these early scenes the apologetic element in the fiction is muted. The novelist's attempt to save Shylock from his fate has not yet come into play; rather, despite a certain literalism and need to rationalize, the author opens up a new sense of what is possible in the story. It is when Lewisohn pries Shylock loose from Venice that his storytelling starts to be deadened by a narrowly ideological impulse. The narrative becomes too transparently a vehicle for Lewisohn's polemical message, including both a fierce sense of the psychological and spiritual costs of Jewish assimilation and an ardent Zionism—things visible in other books he wrote in the 1920s, 1930s, and 1940s, including his autobiographical novel, *The Island Within* (1928), and his reflections on the Jewish Diaspora, *Israel* (1925). In *The Last Days of Shylock*, for example, Joseph Nasi puts his friend in charge of a great, visionary project, that of rebuilding the ruined Roman city of Tiberias in the Holy Land as a refuge for persecuted Jews from Europe and the Middle East, creating there a commercial and a scholarly center. The project is in the end thwarted by both internal conflicts and the intrigues of native Arabs and Christians, as well as by the plotting of Nasi's rivals in the Sultan's court. This story, again based on historical sources, gives us a Shylock who not only shares the trials of the Diaspora, but also finds his way to Israel and to participation in some early shadow of Zionism. This is given a more mystical coloring when, on his way to Tiberias, Shylock passes close to the town of Safed, the home of an important Kabbalistic school. His caravan loses its way in the desert but is led to safety by the great scholar and synthesizer Moses Cordovero, the teacher of Isaac Luria, whose work was the foundation of so much modern Kabbalism and Hassidism. Cordovero appears and departs in silence, like a ghost. Shylock's travels make clear to him the threat of Islamic antisemitism, the dangers even of this place of refuge, the impossibility of rebuilding Tiberias, yet these recognitions somehow only gesture toward the better though still vexed hopes of the twentieth century.

Lewisohn wants to cure Shakespeare's Jew of his painful isolation and to give a nobler explanation for his rage, freeing him from the taint of miserliness, murderousness, and monstrosity. Yet the attempt to save Shylock both empties out Shakespeare's character and collapses Lewisohn's real, if fragile, acts of historical imagination and wonder. It is telling that Lewisohn, in removing Shylock from Venice and Europe, acts to save him from the consequences of his forced conversion, sparing him the dangers, guilt, and complicities of the double life he might have lived as a Christian in Venice. The effect is to save Shylock at the cost of undoing his puzzling interior life, which is part of what makes him so powerful for us. In taking Shylock out of Venice and out of the limbo in which Shakespeare left him after the trial, Lewisohn produces instead a straw man, a mere puppet or passive witness. The impulse to give us a real, historical Jew instead of an antisemitic grotesque yields only a different kind of grotesque. The weakly idealizing motives that drive the latter half of the novel come through most clearly in the way it resolves the story of Shylock's lost daughter. Joseph Nasi sends Shylock to Cyprus after its conquest by the Turks, in order to act as his agent. There, among a group of Jews he ransoms from a Greek pirate, captives about to be sold into slavery, he discovers his daughter Jessica, accompanied by her three young sons. Jessica tells the story of how Lorenzo, a truly loving husband after all, yet an aristocratic wastrel, was betrayed by the envious Bassanio. Moving through the years from city to city and court to court, falling more deeply into debt, he can never quite escape his own residual hatred of his wife's Jewish origins, and after years of wandering abandons her, falling into the service of a foreign army. Shylock forgives his daughter, though not before she acknowledges her own injustice and her failure to understand her father's charitable work, the pious reasons for his house's austerity. Jessica's sons are all immediately circumcised, and Shylock names them (with a slight smile, we are told) Abraham, Isaac, and Jacob. Shakespeare's Jew is allowed to live out his last years peacefully in Istanbul surrounded by his family, watching Abraham's astonishing successes as a Talmudic scholar, conscious of events that speak of the continued dangers that beset the Jews in Europe and Asia, but consoled by his own kind of Kabbalism, which seeks for truth not on earth but in an ideal, immaterial world.

The novel seeks to restore a Shylock who is of use to the Jewish people, a point of help, identification, and less troubled sympathy, Shylock the patriarch and wise man, Shylock the *tzaddik*. Lewisohn's Shylock is never anything else than a proud, faithful Jew, a public leader and secret ally of the oppressed, one whose anger has the force of a just, collective rage rather than a singular and fiercely ambiguous resentment. The novel has its more reflective moments, admittedly, as when it speaks of the mystery of Christian hatred or the dangers of Jewish messianism, the false hopes and distortions of thought these bring into play. Lewisohn can be stark not only about the survival of this one Jew but about the mysterious survival of antisemitism. Yet he gives us, for the most part, a good golem to replace the bad golem that Shylock has become in European memory. And as happens with golems, the would-be savior turns out to be as dangerous as he is helpful. One sees all that is lost or evaded in this particular act of solidarity. Shylock the wit, the playful, even self-destructive actor disappears; Shylock the revenger disappears; Shylock with his secrets disappears, his extremity of rage, his glee in challenging those to whom he speaks, throwing their hatred back into their ears. There is no such wild malice in Lewisohn's Shylock as might make other Jews who had gathered in the courtroom flee in terror when he begins to speak, running back to the ghetto to warn their fellow Jews of a potential pogrom (something that was suggested in two recent productions of *Merchant* that I saw). The unaccountable, singular being who is Shakespeare's Shylock would simply not recognize himself in the novel; he would see Lewisohn's Shylock as rather a weird impostor.

Heinrich Heine's way of finding a later history and voice for Shylock is the more sharply true for keeping him closer to home. The exiled poet gives us a Shylock who has never left Venice, surviving there to the writer's own time in a ghostly fashion. However willful his fiction, Heine does not flee from his own bafflement and sense of conflict, nor does he try to save Shylock from his fate. Rather he sees that fate at once more inwardly and more historically, taking stock of what remains unknowable.

The section entitled "Jessica," in Heine's *Shakespeare's Girls and Women* (1838), begins with an account of the author's visit to the Drury Lane theater in London to watch the Shylock of Edmund Kean. Heine would write elsewhere, in letters published in the *Allgemeine Theater-Revue* (1838), about the eerie force of Kean's performance, his varied naturalness of utterance, the sense he gave of a man caught up in the web of his own words. He describes how, in Shylock's "cur" speech in act 1, the actor's "keen eyeballs peered weirdly and frighteningly. . . . His voice too is submissive at that instant, only faintly one hears in it his sullen rancour; but his eyes cannot dissemble, incessantly they shoot forth their poisoned arrows." In "Jessica" Heine's attention is stolen by a different voice and different eyes, those of a female spectator at the back of his theater box, "a pale British beauty who, at the end of the fourth Act, wept passionately, and many times cried out, 'The poor man is wronged!' It was a countenance of the noblest Grecian cut, and its eyes were large and black. I have never been able to forget them, those great black eyes which wept for Shylock!" This displaced voicing of sympathy and protest (which knowingly risks sentimentality), leads into a broader reflection on the play and its sources, and on the question of who or what is wronged. The play is for Heine a tragedy, showing Shakespeare's genius in drawing a picture of a suffering human being out of the crude materials of antisemitic fable, "the hatred of the lower and the higher mob." Alongside the malice of the Christians, he marks Jessica's moral cowardice, and that appetite for gold and social position which makes her content to abet Christian slanders of her father. (Her one redeemable moment, Heine thinks, comes in the abduction scene, when she worries about how the torch which Lorenzo asks her to carry will make more visible her shameful transformation into a boy: "What, must I hold a candle to my shames?" It is a slight trace of what he sees as the essential reserve, chastity, and inwardness of the Jewish spirit, something that shows "the deep affinity . . . between these two ethical nations, Jews and Old Germans.") For Heine, the source of Christian hatred is not easy to pinpoint. Early on in the essay he quotes a long letter that he says he received from a friend—a letter almost certainly invented by Heine himself—which argues that such hatred is grounded less in religious than in social differences. The drama "in reality exhibits neither Jews nor Christians, but oppressors and oppressed, and the madly agonized jubilation of the latter when they can repay their arrogant tormentors with interest for insults inflicted on them." The letter argues that modern antisemitism inherits from the Middle Ages a hatred that the common people directed against Jewish moneylenders, but that should properly have been turned against both the aristocracy and the Catholic Church, who made the Jews their tool and their scapegoat. The ground of the hatred is thus real but finds the wrong object. It is a hatred that continues to be directed (or misdirected) against Jewish bankers and merchants in an age of increasing industrialization (though Heine is never as viciously reductive as his friend Karl Marx, who in his essay "On the Jewish Question," bluntly identifies Jewishness with the blind forces of capitalism). Heine's historical and ideological analysis seems to take him only so far, however; he finds himself drawn to a more concrete and more ambiguous reimagining of the play. He seems moved to this partly by the haunting cry of that English beauty, who for all the noble Grecian cut of her face seems a displaced version of Shylock's dark-eyed Jewish daughter, and who asks for a deeper account of Shylock's being wronged. We also feel Heine's need to probe his own conflicted fascination with the paradox of Shylock, with a mania and rage that seem essential to his being; there is something in Shylock's monstrosity that can't be made sense of as merely an ugly error of the oppressed. Shylock draws Heine because the character puts to the test his own characteristic love for playing—critically, comically, but also religiously—with antisemitic stereotypes. As Jeffrey L. Sammons suggests, Heine's vision of the world is most challenging when he probes his own wounds. "He deliberately chose the hard case," writes John Gross.

Under the heading "Portia," Heine moves into a largely fictive autobiographical anecdote. Heine tells of a recent trip to Venice during which he went in search of Shylock, convinced that Shakespeare's Jew must still remain in the streets or squares of the city, so vividly had the playwright imagined him there. The report begins on a satirical note. Heine first searches for him at the Rialto, in order, he writes, to give him the news that his descendant, "M. de Shylock of Paris . . . has become the most powerful baron in Christendom and has been decorated by His Most Catholic Majesty of Spain with the Order of Isabella, founded to celebrate the expulsion from Spain of the Jews and the Moors." (It is Baron James de Rothschild who is meant, as S. S. Prawer notes, a man whom Heine commonly treats with respect, if also occasionally barbed humor, unlike other Jewish bankers, including members of his own family, whom he can readily refer to as "Shylocks.") When he does not find Shylock in the place of commerce, Heine looks for him in the old ghetto. Here the narrative takes a turn into something more plangent and eerie:

The Jews happened just then to be celebrating their sacred Day of Atonement and stood wrapped in their white prayer shawls with uncanny noddings of their heads, looking like an assembly of ghosts. There they stood, these poor Jews, fasting and praying, since early morning; they had tasted neither food nor drink since the evening before, and had also begged the forgiveness of all their acquaintances for any evil things they might have said of them during the past year so that God might pardon them too—a beautiful custom, which exists, strangely enough, among people who have, we are told, remained strangers to the teachings of Christ. . . . But while, looking around for old Shylock, I passed all these pale, suffering Jewish faces in review, I made a discovery which—alas!—I cannot suppress. I had visited the madhouse of San Carlo that same day, and now it occurred to me, in the synagogue, that in the glances of the Jews there flickered the same dreadful, half-staring and half-unsteady, half-crafty and half-stupid expression which I had seen shortly before in the eyes of the lunatics in San Carlo.

Eyes again, not showing the pity and protest of the woman at the theater, or the flashing, knowing intensity of Kean, but something more uncertain, a wounded, baffled knowledge and guile, mixed with fear, illusion, and stupidity. Heine writes that the indescribable look in the inmates' eyes was in fact the token of the mind's subordination to a fixed idea. In the case of the Jews in the Venetian synagogue, it is faith "in that extra-mundane thunder-God." If that faith has a touch of madness, he acknowledges that it yet carried the Jews through immensities of earthly suffering and martyrdom, the memories of which they carry "tied onto them with sacred leather thongs." That look is also a mark of the Jews' attachment to the merely doctrinal differences and wanton shibboleths that keep them from finding common cause with Christians and Moslems, who share, he says, the same essential moral truths, set at odds with a buried paganism. Heine cannot be in doubt about the historical reasons for Jews' keeping aloof from the other religions; and he is often fiercely satiric about the ambitions and failures of assimilation. Yet his sense of the failures of solidarity that he maps out in the essay leads him to a dire prophecy. The Christian church,

CHAPTER ELEVEN

he writes, however vicious its persecutions of the Jews, has its own
investment in keeping them alive, partly as witnesses to its historical supersession of Old Testament religion. "But if one day Satan,
or sinful pantheism (from which all the saints of the Old and New
Testaments and of the Koran may preserve us!), should conquer,
there will gather over the heads of the poor Jews a tempest of persecution that will far surpass all they have had to endure before."
Germany, he tells us in *On the History of Religion and Philosophy in
Germany* (1835), "is the most fruitful soil for pantheism." Such pantheism, or what Heine elsewhere calls sensualism, is yet no essential evil, rather it is something made Satanic by a religious idealism;
it speaks for bodily, worldly impulses lent their destructive power
by the very fearful religious purity, the Gnostic impulse, that slanders them as sinful and thus takes revenge upon them.

Here again Heine may trouble us by making believing Jews
complicit in their own status as victims; it is hard to read his tone,
which mixes the comic and the menacing, the prophetic and the
mock-prophetic, the sordid and the spiritual. An almost masochistic delight breaks through in such moments of Heine's writing.
(Consider here a poem from 1844, commemorating the dedication
of a new hospital for needy Jews in Hamburg, where he praises the
donor—his uncle Solomon, always conflicted in his generosity toward the poet—for seeking to cure poverty and illness, yet adds
that Jewishness itself is an incurable disease, the one plague the
children of Israel carried with them when they were taken out of
Egypt.) As often in his work, Heine stands both inside and outside
the circle of the Jewish people, playing out what bitter knowledge
the types of antisemitism yield him. From this prophecy of Jewish
destruction we find our way back to the story of the poet's search
for Shakespeare's Jew. The essay ends thus:

Though I looked all around in the synagogue of Venice, I could not see
the face of Shylock anywhere. And yet it seemed to me that he must be
there, hidden under one of those white robes, praying more fervently

than any of his fellow believers, with stormy wildness, even with madness, to the throne of Jehovah, the stern divine monarch. I did not see
him. Towards evening, however, when, as the Jews believe, the gates
of heaven are closed and no further prayer can enter, I heard a voice in
which tears flowed that were never wept from human eyes. . . . It was a
sobbing that might have moved a stone to pity. . . . These were sounds
of agony that could come only from a heart that held locked within it
all the martyrdom which a tormented people had endured for eighteen
centuries. . . . And it seemed to me that I knew this voice well; I felt as
though I had heard it long ago, when it lamented, with the same tone
of despair: "Jessica, my child!"

Heine is powerful in describing the breaking forth of such ghostly
voices, knowing their emergence from buried need and pain. So in
his early poem "Almansor" (1825), we hear dark, shattering murmurs coming from the columns of the great mosque in Cordoba
after it has been reconsecrated as a church by triumphant Christian
Spain, cries of resentment that he imagines bringing down the
building itself. (Both the cries and the vision of destruction emerge,
we learn, from the unconscious fantasy of the moor Almansor, disappointed and guilt ridden after having accepted baptism for love of
a Christian maid, one whose grateful tears mingle their dampness
with that of the holy water.) In the late poem, "Jehuda ben Halevy,"
from *Hebrew Melodies* (1851), the poet hears buzzing in his head an
"elegiac whining, humming like a kettle"; it is, he realizes, an echo
of the complaint of the Israelite captives in Psalm 137, the psalm
of exile, that ends with an address to the "daughter of Babylon,"
blessing the man who "dasheth thy little ones against the stones."
That psalm resonates with the poet's own Job-like rage even as
he uses it to conjure up the spectral memory of the great Jewish
poet of medieval Andalusia, martyred (according to legend) on a
pilgrimage to Jerusalem. In "Portia," Heine describes the Venetian
synagogue so that Shylock himself remains unseen, unnamed, set
apart from the prayers of those visible Jews, whose murmurings

cannot match this voice of stormy wildness, even madness. The voice speaks for both a communal and a personal sorrow; it prays, if at all, to a closed heaven, speaking to no God. The scene is all the stranger given Heine's insistent literalism about Shylock's sorrow, and his imagining of a lament that responds, at a distance, to the voice of the grave English beauty whom he describes at the outset of his essay, the redeemed double of Jessica. The voice that cries "Jessica, my child" choruses with that of the young woman who cries "The poor man is wronged," as if reconciling the two speakers within his own memory, matching their very different sorrows.

Why is one golem different from other golems? Why is one reimagining of a Shakespearean character stronger, more searching than another? It lies in an inventiveness, a surprise, that acknowledges the power of the original work, sending us back to it more sharply, even as that revision risks being cut off and isolated. Heine can be sentimental enough, and grossly polemical; for all his wit there also is a fundamentally religious bent to his evocation entirely absent from Shakespeare's play. Yet he has joined himself more strongly to the spirit of the play than Lewisohn, while shifting it on its axis. He provides a version of Shylock's survival that stitches him more deeply back into the play's ambivalences. He wants Shylock's voice to continue, somehow, after the trial, in all its pathos, refusing an easy cure; it provides, for one thing, a point of purchase for Heine's own vexed relation to his Jewish inheritance. What differentiates this from Lewisohn's fiction is not just Heine's distinct theories about Jewish history or the logic of antisemitism. It depends as much on Heine's way of keeping faith with, taking the measure of, the paradoxes of Shakespeare's Shylock. He figures a sorrow that has no answer in history, yet keeps on being spoken, reminding us of Shylock's own opacity, his mania, his uncanny compulsiveness. Heine marks Shylock's isolation even from his own community of Jews, among whose prayers his voice speaks a more private sorrow, however soaked in history. Heine's is a willful fantasy of Shylock's survival, knowing the willfulness of Shakespeare's. That survival's ghostly power, something that in Heine both is and isn't a specifically Jewish power of survival, gains its authority by being staked on what remains so stark a fiction, Shakespeare's story of an imaginary Jew in an imaginary Venice, the work of an author who knew nothing about the ghetto, about the Day of Atonement, or about Jewish mythologies of prayer.

Let me note here one last instance of Shylock's afterlife. It speaks to what Shakespeare's fiction makes possible, to the question of what a later artist can draw from within it. If there is a romance version of Shylock, a reversing mirror of the Jewish genius of deprivation, it might be best exemplified by the figure of Uncle Isak in Ingmar Bergman's 1982 film *Fanny and Alexander*. It is set in the Swedish city of Uppsala, in the first decade of the twentieth century. Isak Jacobi is a Jewish moneylender and junk dealer, also, we learn early on, a friend and former lover of the matriarch of the Ekdahl family, once a great actress and grandmother to the film's eponymous children. We encounter Isak first as little more than a charming guest at a family Christmas party (he is "uncle" only by adoption and love), but as the film unfolds he reveals more secret resources. His crucial act is to rescue Fanny and Alexander when they have, with their mother Emilie, become the virtual captives of a chillingly cruel Lutheran bishop whom Emilie married a year after the death of her first husband, a touchingly hapless actor and theater manager. (Emilie, herself an actress, had in her grief sought refuge from the world of changing masks and found to her dismay a man with a single, blind mask of purity fused onto his face.) Isak spirits the children from the desolate house of the bishop by a curious trick: he arrives at the house to buy an antique chest, in order discretely to alleviate a "financial embarrassment" without the bishop's having to borrow money directly from the Jew. At an opportune moment, when the bishop has gone off to count his money and write a receipt, Isak finds the children and hides them inside that very chest, covering them with a large black cloth. The bishop returns, and Isak opens the chest to show him he is taking nothing not his own. The bishop seems to see nothing there. Yet he still suspects Isak of an attempt at kidnapping, at cheating him of "his" children, and calls the moneylender a "damned, filthy, loathsome Jewish swine," striking Isak repeatedly until the bishop's sister restrains him. (Isak, left alone and on his knees, lets out a cry of rage to heaven; a light falls on his face and a white flash blanks out the screen.) Bergman in his picture of Isak translates and redeems the hidden sense of Shylock as a kind of magician; Isak's power speaks for a generosity at once linked to and exceeding his wealth—a good use of riches that counters the austerity of the self-tormenting bishop, who seeks only to dominate the souls of others. This Jew's casket conceals lost children, stolen back to their home, rather than holding gold or jewels stolen from the Jew's home by a selfish daughter.

The ambiguity of Isak's powers is made clearer by what we see of his house, where the children are kept safe. It is a labyrinth of old furniture, art, curios, clothes, and books; there is a breathing mummy as well as a theater of beautiful puppets made by Isak's nephew, Aron. Another, more mysterious inhabitant of the house is Aron's brother, Ismael, a scholar and even a clairvoyant, yet someone who is kept in a locked room as if to protect him or others from danger. For Alexander, Bergman's alter ego in the film— we have earlier seen him playing with a toy theater and a magic lantern—Isak's house is an education in specters, simulacra, and dreams. Wandering the house at night, he glimpses the ghost of his father, who offers an apology for his failure to protect his children. The boy also converses fearfully and mockingly with the voice of God, a voice that turns out to belong to one of Aron's gigantic puppets. Aron then shows him into the chamber of Ismael, who takes Alexander aside and—in a remarkable scene, half seduction and half mutual trance—evokes the boy's hatred for his stepfather, asking him to acknowledge that hatred even as Ismael seems to lend it substance. We see on-screen Alexander's malicious fantasy as it becomes an actual event, a nightmarish scene in which the bishop is burned alive by his own moribund sister, who accidentally sets herself alight with a lamp and throws herself on her brother: "a horrible scream echoing through the house, a shapeless burning figure moving across the floor—shrieking." Bergman opens up the unseen spaces of Shylock's house. The Jew's designs are given a new face; his riches and powers become something like those of Prospero. Isak's house is a refuge, also a place of dangerous revelation and trickery. He is a maker and keeper of golems, including a puppet Yahweh; those in his house help give life to Alexander's fear and resentment as well as his love, exposing buried terrors. Transformative as it is, this house is not a place Alexander can live in for longer than an interval, like the "little world" of his dead father's theater. Nor can the enchantments of Uncle Isak keep at bay the ghost of the bishop, who steals upon Alexander toward the end of the film, striking him to the ground, telling the boy, "You can't escape me."

Chapter Twelve

A DREAM

I am sitting in the orchestra of an old theater, close to the stage. I think that I must be in the front row, but it turns out to be the second. The seats are reversed so that one can see the audience comfortably, the stage only by twisting one's body around and resting one's chin on the back of the seat. There are high balconies, a red velvet curtain framed by gilded scrollwork, and cracked plaster walls with fading frescoes of gods and nymphs. The audience gathers slowly. The low hum of talk increases. A tall man in uniform stands looking down from one of the boxes, his eyes in shadow. Beside him sits his mother, who says something I cannot hear about a man seated near me, an actor I know, a great comedian, who rushes from his seat and leaves by a back door as the houselights fall.

We are called to attention by a sound from the pit. The curtain rises on a street scene, a city square surrounded by tall, precariously raised buildings joined together at a height by frail bridges. From a narrow alley, an old man enters, dressed in rags, hunchbacked and shrunken, a gargoyle cracked free from its perch. He walks uneasily, doubtful of finding his way, kneeling down now and then to write with his fingers on the paving stones. He murmurs to himself. "Things, rings, kings, strings. You knew it, none more than you. Look to her. Let him look to his bond. None of mine. The bird has flown, shut it in the ground. Dust agape. Breed there. Is the sea a sea a sea? These Christian husbands. Yis, yis, yis." A crowd of children trails after him, shouting "Gobbo! Gobbo!" scattering when he turns toward them with a shout. From another street enters a procession of young girls clad in formal black attire, their faces have a piercing sweetness. Each carries in her hands an open box containing a mummified heart. The man runs at one of them and finds himself wrestling with air.

The scene changes, there is a wide, rising meadow that drops off sharply at its highest end, forming a cliff that falls to a rocky shore. A rush of noise fills the air, and one looks down dizzily at swelling masses of wave. When it strikes the broken stones, the water bursts into foam, it makes irregular arcs of mist, runs in white rivers between the piled boulders, or sifts in slow, threaded patterns over the surface of the green, receding waves. Scattered throughout the meadow are groups of spotted sheep, some of which run as if possessed over the edge of the cliff, tumbling onto the rocks, their woolly shapes lapped at by tongues of white foam. A horde of monkeys dives at the carcasses, pulling from inside them bells, knives, crowns, and tiny human skulls.

The old man walks now along the base of the cliff. Gold hoops hang from his ears, his long garment is decked all over with wild flowers. He begins to dance among the animals, living and dead, slowly at first, then with abandon. His motions are like the motions of the sea, shadows cast by his moving shoulders fall on all that lies around him.

A message is being sent to me as I sit in the audience. The courier is waiting for the play to end, pacing back and forth in the lobby, longing to break through into the darkened auditorium, to run down the aisle and find me where I sit, whispering the message in my ear. It is a message from the actor onstage; he has invited me back to his dressing room when the play is over, we are old friends and have not seen each other in years, he caught sight of me from the wings and now he must talk to me, it is all that is on his mind as he dances there onstage.

I look up at the ceiling of the auditorium, which is faintly lit with a swarm of lamps, less like stars in the night sky than street-lights seen from above. They begin to flicker, sputter, and then fall. I think that I might in time repair them, I even imagine the scaffold on which I would crawl, slowly moving from lamp to lamp, making each right, probing the old wiring and relays, screwing each new, pristine bulb into its tiny socket until the network of lights was whole again. I get up from my seat, make my way across the heads of those behind me as if floating or swimming, they buoy me up as I try to reach the backstage door. All I can hear in the dark is the clink of the old man's earrings.

Chapter Thirteen

ESTHÉTIQUE DU MAL

It is hard to settle one's questions about Shylock. Shakespeare has invented in him a peculiarly tough kind of puzzle, resistant yet drawing energy into it like a black hole. He must have wanted that. Shylock does not organize revelations about himself as other of Shakespeare's major characters do, partly because of how he is both cast out and yet stays present at the end of the play. John Hollander writes of the history of scholarly commentary on him that "every added bit of critical insight only tends to collect in the pool of indeterminacy, rather than to open a sluice out of it."

One question that sticks in my mind has to do with the larger conceptual powers of the play. Does *The Merchant of Venice* point to an antisemitic or anti-Judaic impulse, a distorting prejudice against Jewish tradition, that stands inescapably at the heart of Christianity, especially the tradition of Christian thought that is shaped by the writings of Saint Paul? I am thinking of the divisive logic of Paul's vision of Jewish tradition, his reappropriations of Jewish symbolism and his hyperbolic, reductive pictures of Jewish Law, especially his evocation of both the Law's impotence and its powers of condemnation; he points to its "evil-mindedness," as Hans Jonas says, and its links to the realm of the demonic. Seeing the world in terms of fierce dualisms—Law against Grace, Old Testament letter versus New Testament spirit—Paul invariably projects the unredeemed half of each dualism onto the Jews. If the history and covenant of Israel form the inescapable precursors to his mission, he appropriates these by making their significance metaphorical rather than literal, making their signs inward rather than embodied (for example, "circumcision is that of the heart" [Romans 2:29]). In the process, he also obscures the anticipations of such an inward turn in Hebrew prophetic tradition. In Paul and the church fathers, the Hebrew Bible's pictures of Israel's faithlessness, idolatry, and hardness of heart, its sufferings and exile— things that for the prophets formed part of a larger process of self-criticism and repentance—are isolated and elaborated in order to describe unchanging aspects of Jewishness. Reading the trial scene in *Merchant*, one can feel Shakespeare reminding us of the dramatic occasions for the Pauline dialectic, its anxious projections and contingent simplifications. Portia's all-too-apparent manipulations of the oppositions of law and mercy or sin and promise, for example, suggest the more political aspects of Pauline thinking. One feels there the violence that can inhabit Pauline spiritualization, though Portia's speeches can also remind one of Paul's reimagining of the grounds of spiritual affiliation and hermeneutic freedom. The play suggests how the oppositional logic of Pauline typology helps to contain even as it gives form to both fear and guilt; this includes fear of Christian tradition's intimate links to the very Jewish scripture it condemns and guilt over the violence it directs against living Jews. On this small stage, we get a picture of how the figure of the alien, legalistic, vengeful, and demonic Jew might serve to localize doubts—including anxieties about the church's priority, universality, and doctrinal authority—that both church leaders and individual believers could not bear to see as internal to church tradition itself, especially at moments of institutional crisis. For Luther, to take just one example, Jews were not simply historical precursors in the history of the Gospel. At one moment, he saw them as stark mirrors of the situation of faithful Christians under threat of divine judgment; at others, he saw them as "precise coordinates for charting evil's invasion of the church." Extending if not deforming Pauline allegorical terms, Luther could use the Jew to define a category of being that includes under its accusatory logic Catholic idolaters and Protestant heretics as much as practicing Jews themselves. Shylock, though resisting allegorical reduction as a character within the play, can point us to such tensions within the history of Christianity. The dramatic struggle to contain and judge Shylock helps suggest how the doctrinally grounded image of the Jew might all too readily become the occasion for literal violence as well as more fantastic fictions. Among those fictions is the late medieval legend of the Wandering Jew, a common shoemaker named Ahasuerus, who in punishment for having mocked Jesus as he carried his cross through the streets of Jerusalem is condemned to remain on earth until the Last Judgment, a testimony to both Jewish hatred of Jesus and Jesus's mixed powers of condemnation and forgiveness. The myth provides a stark image of Jews' paradoxical condition, in Augustine's formula, as witnesses both to Christian truth and to their own iniquity.

The dramatic shapes of the play, its structures of mirroring and projection, equally illuminate more modern accounts of antisemitic hatred, in particular, the idea that the insidious, secret, and rootless power and malice attributed to Jews are in fact rationalizing projections of qualities in the antisemite himself, a mirror of his fear of things idiosyncratic, unaligned, and difficult to assimilate. This hidden work of projection is one reason why, as Theodor Adorno and Max Horkheimer argue, the dangerous Jew of European antisemitism combines in himself aspects at once archaic and sophisticated, irrational and hyperrational. Jean-Paul Sartre pictures the antisemite as a person turned to stone by his need for imperious, impenetrable convictions, displacing onto the Jew his unacknowledged fears of a volatile, contingent world. And Sartre's Jew, like Shylock, is himself haunted by the identity imposed on him by Christian hate, forced to assume a phantom personality at once strange and familiar, feeding on the very hatred that threatens him, always seeing himself through the eyes of others. (For Sartre, indeed, the antisemite creates the Jew.) There are also moments in *The Merchant of Venice* that evoke Hannah Arendt's picture in *The Origins of Totalitarianism* of both the arbitrariness of antisemitic hatred and its lunatic logic, its opportunistic errors about the causes of danger in the world, its way of fitting its lies to certain real truths about the place of Jews in history. For Arendt, the figure of the hated Jew gives form to what isn't there as well to what is, one reason that antisemitism becomes for her a type of more general impulses of hatred. Her picture suggests why, from one angle of view, all antisemitism is antisemitism without Jews, a hatred of nonexistent things. At the same time, Arendt offers a provocative, even bitter commentary on the ways that assimilated Jews in nineteenth-century Europe made themselves vulnerable to prejudice through their own self-flattering, contradictory, and emptily abstract myths of Jewish difference—myths challenged, she argues, by Jews like Heine, Bernard Lazare, and Kafka, who made themselves into "conscious pariahs," knowingly embracing the role of intransigent alien forced upon them by Christian society.

Arendt's book shows how the literary fictions of writers like Marcel Proust, Joseph Conrad, Rudyard Kipling, and Kafka serve as superior registers for comprehending the structure of hatred that shapes modern ideologies of imperialism and totalitarianism. These writers help her catch the intimate human strangeness and surprise of such hatred, and even what its forms may keep of human love. They speak to what George Kateb describes as Arendt's demand that we try to imagine, as far as our resources allow, the inward life of those we see as monsters, "the ways in which they saw and felt the world." The imaginative effort of Arendt's authors, humanizing creators of fiction, becomes an ironic mirror image of that life-denying imposition of unreality that for Arendt constitutes the work of totalitarianism. Her book in turn gives us, as readers of *The Merchant of Venice*, lessons in philosophical and moral tact, helping to sort out what wisdom we can gain from the play. But there is a limitation in thus using Arendt's book or *The Merchant of Venice*. Whether we want to see the play as implicated in anti-semitic ideologies and myths, or as subtly exposing them, laying bare their logic, such analyses may give us a narrowed picture of what is at stake in its representations. As I have said, I am not sure that Shakespeare was very interested in Jews or antisemitic hatred apart from how they might help him construct a particular kind of dramatic machine. If he counted on his original audience's malice toward his imaginary Jew, he also draws its interest toward other sorts of conflict. The problem of figuring out what the play tells us about the ideological uses of the Jew depends on how one takes Shylock's generality and particularity, the way his energy explodes past all restraints of the comic form. If the play points to a critique of Christian antisemitism, that critique is part of something larger and yet more local. Too often it feels as if the mere taking of sides in the struggle between Shylock and his enemies is the essential thing for critics; it is inevitable that we ask, to put it crudely, whether the play is pro-Shylock or anti-Shylock, but that gets the question wrong. Art doesn't work that way. I have suggested that Shylock turns the antisemitic hatred of the Christians back upon them, stealing their projections for himself, making of these a mirror and a weapon, even as he mingles with them his own reactive rage and sense of loss. Ideological affiliation is not the issue here. One feels the centripetal force of Shakespeare's representation, how it pushes toward blank, opaque uncertainty, a different and more difficult to place unreason, a troubling pleasure and wonder. That riddling representation is one of the play's weird charities.

George Santayana spoke of Shakespeare as a poet with an acute metaphysical capacity but no real interest in religion—religion being, for this philosopher, an impulse toward the consecration of life by a unifying faith and a clear vision of forces above the human that are yet its environment and aim. I think that judgment remains

broadly right about the work, even if Santayana's sense of religion
has its limits. The fact that *The Merchant of Venice* is a play which so
sharply engages questions about religious faction and the ambigui-
ties of biblical interpretation does not refute Santayana's picture.
It rather suggests some of the play's stark ironies. Shakespeare so
broadens his representation of Christian hatred of Jews, suggesting that hatred's more divided, intimate, and coercive purposes,
its wild opportunism in appeals to both mercy and law, that it is
hard to make the play serve a strictly confessional end or to see it as
taking sides in an institutional or doctrinal debate. The forms and
feelings of religious life remain tied inescapably to the secular, to a
drama of human purposes, however uncanny or preternatural these
purposes are at times. Even what feels sacred is mixed up with the
profane, if not with sacrilege. The analysis of human hatred both
possesses and goes beyond the domain of the religious. The complexity of Shakespeare's vision comes, for one thing, from the fact
that it is so involved with our understanding of the theatricality of
Shylock, and our sense of how Shylock is a mirror for the poet's own
ambivalences about his art. Again, one of the tasks of understanding the play is to get at the intertwined particularity and generality
of its picture of Shylock, and the hatred he arouses. James Shapiro's
Shakespeare and the Jews, for example, explores how the figure of
the Jew preoccupied Elizabethan authors; it shows in detail how
ideas of Jewish ambiguity, alienness, malice, and duplicity helped
to shape by contrast an emergent image of pure English Christian
nationhood, even in a world where actual Jews were scarce. The
threat to such purity came especially from the way that Jews were
supposed always to slip across clear religious, political, racial, and
even gender lines—something visible, say, in the common suspicion that all Jewish converts were in fact marranos, practicing
their old faith in secret. Throughout this study, so strongly staked
against any idea of an "eternal antisemitism," *The Merchant of Venice*
serves Shapiro as a powerful analytic tool. It works like radar to
help him focus on certain fantasies of Jewish menace—ritual mur-

der or castration—or apocalyptic wishes for Jewish conversion, that haunt Elizabethan England, and the play itself. Yet even as Shapiro's book brings out so richly the historical and critical stakes of Shakespeare's play, it is often hard to hear amid his myriad examples the distinct note of Shylock's voice, his rage or doubt or obsession. One misses the play's more idiosyncratic hints about the origins and dramatic metamorphoses of antisemitic hatred, and the ways such hatred can be turned back against those who speak it.

Norman Rabkin usefully stresses the play's ardent refusal to take sides between Christians and Jews, arguing that its power lies rather in a constant oscillation of perspectives. But even this moderate formulation gives up the game too quickly, or simply gets the game wrong, since what is most troubling in the play cannot be made sense of by framing or denying a parti pris. There is a quality of interest in Shylock which neither side of the debate, insofar as they can be isolated, could bear to appropriate or even know how to appropriate. This is part of what I meant by speaking of the play as an experiment in the poetics of repugnancy. Shylock's refusal to evade his own repugnancy forces others to reveal themselves or hide themselves more deeply. In a situation like this, taking sides can be a way of hiding. It risks substituting a posture of radicality for an understanding of extremity. Angus Fletcher proposed this analogy: Shylock is like the strong kid who cannot be allowed to play the game, the kid who will be chosen by neither side. This is not because he will play the game better or because he will betray the side he's on, but because he will in his strength simply shatter the game as a whole, if he does not expose the fact that the players themselves are playing a different game from what they had supposed, one in which it is not clear what constitutes winning. The Venetians keep playing the game even after Shylock has exposed it because Portia teaches them how to turn it against him.

Such difficulties are why we need to hold on to things hovering in the shadows. The very analytic power of our hermeneutic techniques is likely to make the play transparent, and so invisible, whereas it is often opaque, even as it shows how human beings give forms to things invisible, things not there. *The Merchant of Venice* begins with Antonio articulating the mystery of his sadness:

> In sooth I know not why I am so sad.
> It wearies me, you say it wearies you;
> But how I caught it, found it, or came by it,
> What stuff 'tis made of, whereof it is born,
> I am to learn.
> And such a want-wit sadness makes of me,
> That I have much ado to know myself. (1.1.1–7)

I do not think that Antonio in the end knows any better why he is sad, what stuff his sadness is made of, and what it makes of him—or what, in turn, he makes of it at the trial, in his masochistic displays before Bassanio. By the end, the origins of his hatred for Shylock remain just as hard to locate. In the play that hatred is in no way perceived as a pathology, which is how Antonio perceives his sadness—perhaps one reason why his hatred helps displace that sadness, if not cure it. It's really not very clear in the end what the Venetians find so hateful in Shylock, not even the fact that he so bluntly hates them. Shylock's purpose seems at times that of making himself into a perfect object of their hatred, as if that might force their reasons for hating him into visibility, but it almost has the opposite effect. The play's making visible of hatred also multiplies its disguises and displacements, as Jacob does his sheep. One cannot easily say whether the Venetians themselves really know at last what or whom they hate in Shylock, or through Shylock. Shylock exists partly to frame the difficulty and pleasure of hating, the difficulty of knowing what one hates; his character suggests the ways that a given hatred, or a particular form of hatred, works to conceal other and perhaps truer objects of hate and fear, even other objects of love, from those who hate. The very means, private and public, by which we seek to release the soul from fear may bind it to new, more hidden fears, or bind love itself to fear. This is something that happens all too nakedly in the history of the church, as the Swiss psychoanalyst and Protestant theologian Oskar Pfister argues in his study *Christianity and Fear*, published in 1944. Pfister's probing, unsettling book explores how consistently Christian sects have betrayed the New Testament's radical call for a love that casts out fear, tracing this crucially to the way that human fear is reinforced by a love that is blocked or misdirected, diverted from what are seen as dangerous objects. The church's persecution of Jews, heretics, and witches is only the most visible sign of that betrayal.

The complexity of Shakespeare's picturing of antisemitic hatred may be partly the result of his knowing so little about the historical situation of actual Jews, so little about places in which the more purely figurative antisemitism of his own culture found objects for malice among living communities of Jews. Registering the virulence of that hatred in a place where so few Jews lived, and certainly had no long-established communities, he may have sensed all the more strongly both its phantasmic quality and how it becomes part of what passes for common sense. He might have seen how it is that antisemitism wants its enemy to disappear from a space where that enemy does not really exist; he might have seen more clearly that the objects of its hatred are more imaginary than real (however real the violence that can be provoked by such imagination). One would like to know whether Shakespeare ever talked with any of the small group of conversos that were living in Elizabethan London. They included Italian musicians at court, who had come to England in Henry VIII's time, as well as a number of Portuguese conversos who had sought refuge from the Inquisition, and who were active as merchants, physicians, and diplomats, not to mention spies. (The Portugese converso Roderigo Lopez, for example, chief physician to Elizabeth, was deeply implicated in Anglo-Spanish espionage, sending secret reports about English foreign policy to Philip II of Spain but apparently working also as a double agent for the English. In 1594 he was tried and convicted of plotting to poison the queen—the truth of the accusation remains in debate—and executed the same year, an event some scholars have seen as a spur to Shakespeare's composition of *The Merchant of Venice*.) It is tempting to imagine some of these persons telling the playwright their stories of persecution, exile, martyrdom, spiritual struggle, or secret religious practice. Such stories might have combined in Shakespeare's imagination with thoughts about the lives of recusant Catholics in England, their fear and nostalgia, their daily experience of secrecy and equivocation in public, and their troubled fascination with martyrdom—things that the poet more certainly knew about, even if the question of his own religious affiliation remains vexed. (I myself find the evidence for Shakespeare's Catholicism thin. But whatever his relation to Catholic thought or worship, or to specific recusant communities, the poet could imagine what it might be like to live in the shadow of a religious mythology at once needful, ruined, and under suspicion, as Stephen Greenblatt explores movingly in his *Hamlet in Purgatory*.) Yet even as we speculate about Shakespeare's acquaintance with actual Jews and Jewish history, we also need to see how much the poet has done without that acquaintance. This too is part of the scandal of the play. A power not only to make something out of nothing but to make a nothing something is one source of the sly shock of Shakespeare's work. It makes description poor; it beggars description. This is an aspect of what is fearful in Shylock, that we cannot place his ground, that a terrible absence and a terrible presence coexist in him.

It is hard to accommodate this blunt power of invention. A measure of the difficulty, the bafflement and anxiety it breeds, can be found in the many theories that someone other than Shakespeare wrote the plays that go under his name. Alternative candidates for authorship are most often persons whose family history, education, or political and ideological affiliations are easier to specify than Shakespeare's, an author whose most powerful acts of making can never be given a clear or sufficient historical foundation. One is not surprised to find writers who argue that a play like *The Merchant of Venice* helps to prove that Shakespeare himself came from a family of English marranos. Such a speculation has the attraction that it so radically cuts through the enigma of the play's vexed partisanship, even as it lends to the play the aura of a secret communication. The idea is indeed no less irrational than the conviction that the plays were written by Francis Bacon or Edward de Vere, earl of Oxford, or even Queen Elizabeth—persons whose authorship seems to make more comprehensible certain aspects of the plays, such as their breadth of learning, their intimate understanding of the work of law and court politics, and their apparent knowledge of foreign nations. I always sense behind such speculations an almost religious fear mixed with a decided literalism and sharp love of conspiracy, as well as a certain snobbery and no doubt an attachment to the plays themselves. I have read a good number of the books, but it is not an easy task. The theories have their fascination; the ingenuity spent on deciphering traces of alternative authorship and explaining how the misattribution took shape is often astonishing. What's most troubling is not their often distorted use of evidence and misplaced historical skepticism, or the fact that they always evade Shakespeare's essential strangeness. It's more that the fear that drives them echoes fears and wishes that drive other, crueler and less self-contained conspiracy theories. Those who ardently deny Shakespearean authorship end up hewing to the wrong sort of secrecy, the wrong sort of mystery and means to solve it.

I have described a Shylock who makes his status as alien or monster into a performance he can turn against his persecutors. This argument might seem merely a way of saving appearances. It spares Shakespeare from being someone who put a crudely antisemitic stereotype onstage and so gave his audience an expected and wholly acceptable public pleasure in hating him. It spares us from having to call Shakespeare an antisemite or the play antisemitic. I do not think my picture of Shylock's motives in the trial scene simply an evasion. The deep, ancient staginess of the evil Jew must have been just what Shakespeare discovered in writing up the trial scene for the stage. A consciousness of the Jew as mask is already implicit in the huge theatrical energy of Marlowe's Barabas, who makes all other religious ideologies reveal themselves as hypocritical or willfully manipulative, and who authenticates his own Machiavellian malice primarily through his theatrical verve and candor. At the same time, what I have described as Shylock's mirroring of his enemies' hatred is not simply a witty, theatrical turn proper only to the Shakespearean stage. That an abused person might thus turn a slander back on those who voice it should come as no surprise. It is a very simple awful wondrous thing. This sort of turning is an example of the all-but-inevitable masks that individuals or groups are forced to assume in the face of a world that enshrines such mythified, empty abuse against them. It is a strategy that can be variously a refuge, a weapon, and a trap. The startling thing is that Shakespeare embeds such a response so complexly, saves it from its isolation, its mere defensiveness. He explores its costs and its pleasures as well as its more public powers, its affiliations with other sorts of performance and its way of challenging its audience.

I keep coming back to the isolation, incompleteness, and reductiveness of Shylock, a status given to him throughout the play, reinforced at the end by his treatment at the trial. Shylock willfully embraces such isolation. In the face of hatred and abuse, he makes a blunt, animalistic cipher of himself, something at once human and inhuman, human in its way of being bound to the inhuman. If he turns this inhumanity on the Christians he also turns it on himself. There is a self-destructive aspect to his posture. Of what more general state of experience is this fervent idiosyncrasy a mirror? In *The Origins of Totalitarianism*, Arendt writes about what it means for a person to lose his human rights, something that for her means losing access to the public sphere which creates real human expression and action, the domain where "action is eloquence," as Volumnia says to Coriolanus. This loss of rights means losing the possibility for that unpredictable, revelatory action that creates a self in the eyes of others, that reveals what a person may indeed not know about himself through mere introspection (both virtues and vices, strengths and weaknesses). Such revelations help the self break free of the automatisms of nature, or what Arendt calls "life processes." For her, this loss of rights and public presence, a condition of totalitarian rule, is likely to coincide with "the instant when a person becomes a human in general . . . *and* different in general, representing nothing but his own absolutely unique individuality which, deprived of expression within and action upon a common world, loses all significance." The loss of rights returns the person to that mere particularity or humanity that arouses "dumb hatred, mistrust, and discrimination" because it points too clearly to "those spheres where men cannot act and change at will." This particularity, the condition of the *idiotes*—the singular or peculiar person rather than the citizen, one who marks "the disturbing miracle contained in the fact that each of us is made as he is"—is sensed as a permanent threat to the public sphere and so becomes the object of its resentment. What is surprising in Shylock, as Shakespeare has framed him, is that he speaks for a mode of revelatory, symbolic action, or exposure to others' judgment, that survives even in a person's being so stripped of his rights and the power of significance. He makes the means of his being stripped into a mask, and thus reclaims them. If he mirrors the modes of action and expression available in the public sphere that excludes his particularity, he also frames these modes of action and expression in a way that the public sphere finds hard to bear. He confronts the public world with the demented mirror of its own arbitrary and unpredictable occasions of representation; he shows it the shapes of its own hatred and, scarily, how these can be repossessed by those it hates. In speeches like the one about the "gaping pig," he embraces the automatisms of will and desire that, Arendt argues, political action tries to cure or banish; he embraces them, takes on the face of that god or animal which, for Aristotle, has no place in the *polis*, and yet insists on staying there, revealing the *polis* to itself even as he is victimized by it.

As *idiotes*, Shylock is a frightening kind of thing. If he shows the public sphere what it mistrusts and hates, he also presents it with the image of a purpose, action, and opinion so uncanny as to skew any more rational accounts of human purpose, action, and opinion. It is a terrible version of freedom. Indeed, he points to an unpredictability, a surprise, that is itself an essential part of the public sphere, including the "inner affinity between the arbitrariness inherent in all [political] beginnings, and human potentialities for crime," as Arendt writes in *On Revolution*. The question of Shylock has a lot to do with what he makes visible and as much with what he drives into invisibility, what he reveals of what cannot be known, but only shown, as Wittgenstein might phrase it.

My use of Arendt here is opportunistic. She is talking about the sort of radical stripping away of rights that occurs under totalitarian regimes, the radical isolation of persons in the world from each other and from their own solitudes. Shylock has the chance at a trial, debate; there are rules and privileges associated with this. Part of what's remarkable is that in his mad embrace of the formality of law (especially in the claims he makes for his bond) he seems to reveal just how fragile his rights under the law are, how incomplete and how isolated he is. He clings to his shred of rights in the face of a public world that leaves him so little space to act; it is a world that seems ready to reinvent and multiply its laws, its constitution, when it needs to express its irrational hatred, making even its mercy a tool for coercion.

Shakespeare always finds his most urgent dramatic forces in such contradictory situations as those of Shylock, in a character's solitude and engagement, his precarious ambition, his combination of exposure and concealment. The poet finds curious spheres of purpose in places where purpose is otherwise lost or deformed, reduced to nothing; he finds new words in places where the terms of the common world have become menacing, contingent, and empty (however much disguised as sense) and yet remain the only material to work with. He finds in such reductions a mutability and a humanness that he can make use of, a property that he can make breed.

So you find the place where Shylock is a king much as my stripped and cast-out Lear is a king.

Chapter Fourteen

OPERATION SHYLOCK

Philip Roth's 1993 novel *Operation Shylock: A Confession* takes place
mostly in and around Jerusalem at the time of the first Palestinian
uprising, or *intifada*, in 1988. The story it tells seems to have little
to do with Shakespeare's fable about a Venetian merchant and a
Jewish moneylender. Shylock is indeed taken up explicitly only
once, in a speech by a man who calls himself David Supposnik, an
Israeli secret policeman disguised as an antiquarian book dealer.
Supposnik reflects angrily on how, through the blunt eloquence of
Shakespeare's words, "the savage, repellent, and villainous Jew, deformed by hatred and revenge, entered as our doppelgänger into the
consciousness of the enlightened West." The mere words "Three
thousand ducats," especially as pronounced with unctuous emphasis by actors like the great Charles Macklin—"Th-th-th-three
th-th-th-thous-s-s-sand ducats-s-s," as one contemporary observer
reported—have become iconic of Shylock's menace. Supposnik's
diatribe is something of a blind, however, being intended mainly
to draw the narrator (Roth himself) into a secret plot, of which
I will say more below. Yet even in the absence of more detailed
references to Shakespeare's play, one senses throughout the novel
Roth's wrestling match with Shylock. Roth explores through wild

and oblique mirrors the nature of Shylock's voice, its disturbing inventiveness, its gleeful and self-wounding powers of rage; we hear at moments the very cadences of Shylock's speeches, his genius for repetition and accumulating grievance. The book touches on the power we feel in Shylock to engage his own status as an object of loathing, on how this disfigures and deludes him, and on how it is fed by larger systems of paranoia, lying, and forgery. The hall of mirrors in which victims and victimizers are caught is central to the book. Crucial also is a sense of the bonds of hatred. Loathing itself becomes a theory, or assumes the mask of theory. The novel also explores, more directly than Shakespeare's play could, what it might mean for a writer to confront a dramatic incarnation of his own authorial ambitions and anxieties.

The problem of doubling is at the heart of the novel, whose central focus is a mysterious creature who calls himself Philip Roth—not the narrator, the living author, but an impostor who has assumed his name. The false Roth comes into view on a visit to Jerusalem, where he is publicly attending the trial of John Demjanjuk, the American autoworker accused of having been "Ivan the Terrible," a vicious camp guard at Treblinka. His principal aim, he explains to the reporters who rush to interview the famous writer, is not to witness the trial but to use the occasion to gather public support for a revolutionary movement called Diasporism. It is a movement that aims to save the Jews of Israel, especially those of European origin, from the twin threats of a second Holocaust at the hands of their Arab enemies and the equally grim fate of becoming themselves oppressors on behalf of an armed Jewish state. To do this, he wants to persuade Israeli Jews to make an exodus *back* to the European countries from which they had fled, returning to "the most authentic Jewish homeland there has ever been, the birthplace of rabbinic Judaism, Hasidic Judaism, Jewish secularism, socialism." Germany, Poland, Austria, Hungary—these countries, burdened by guilt and an acute sense of loss, will now welcome the exiles home: "People will be jubilant. People will be in tears. They will be shouting, 'Our

Jews are back! Our Jews are back!'" It is a program that would restore to Jews the nourishments of a Diaspora that were delusively
curtailed by the Jewish invention of the state of Israel, a state that
is now "deforming and disfiguring Jews as only our anti-Semitic
enemies once had the power to do." As a defense of Jews against
the depredations of antisemitism, Diasporism is a kind of loony,
inverted double of Zionism, an ideology that combines nostalgia
and paranoia, historical blindness and satiric penetration.

Roth hears about the impostor in a phone call from his cousin
Apter in Jerusalem. Apter, a tiny "unborn adult," escaped the death
camps by being put to work by a German officer in a male brothel in
Munich and now supports himself by painting miserable images of
the Holy Land for the tourist trade, always fearful of the violence,
Jewish and Arab, that looms around him. Though Roth at first
wonders if the news is one of Apter's paranoid fantasies, he finds
it confirmed by his friend, the Israeli novelist Aaron Appelfeld.
Roth himself is staying in a hotel suite in New York, struggling
to recover from a breakdown that had been induced by the pain-
killer Halcion—a hundred days of psychic dismemberment, self-
loss, and panic that he fears reflects "something concealed, ob-
scured, masked, suppressed, or maybe simply uncreated in me until
I was fifty-four." He flies to Jerusalem to confront the other Roth
directly. (His cover story is that he must interview Appelfeld, a
writer whose stories about dangerous and desperate forms of Jewish
innocence mark him as another antiself for Roth.) The novel's epi-
graph comes from Genesis, "Then some man wrestled with Jacob
until the break of day." Its most outrageous energy is drawn from
the struggle of the author's fictive self with his impersonator, an
often unspoken and self-wounding yet also hugely comic activ-
ity. The meeting with the false Roth reveals no demon or angel,
but rather something more unsettling. What he finds is a human
monster of resentment, a man with no center of his own, a person
desperately, shamefully in awe of the author whose appearance he
almost perfectly mirrors, "a conventionally better-looking face, a

little less mismade than my own," the Jewish features smoothed out. After his first baffling encounter with this creature at the King David Hotel, Roth broods on what to call him. It is a mistake, he feels, to call him a double, to see in him a version of that "famously real and prestigious archetype . . . incarnating the hidden depravities or the respectable original, as personalities or inclinations that refuse to be buried alive." How can Roth lend this authoritative label to a creature who is an utter genius of unreality, "uncohesive, disappointed, a very shadowy, formless fragmented thing. A kind of wildly delineated nothing"? Searching for a better title, Roth triumphantly dubs his double "Moishe Pipik," after a mischievous imp of Eastern European Jewish folklore, whose name in Yiddish means "Moses Bellybutton." "Moishe Pipik" is a label that had served in Jewish households, Roth tells us, as the nickname for "the kid who pisses in his pants, the someone who is a bit ridiculous, a bit funny, a bit childish, the comic shadow alongside whom we had all grown up," linked to that curious, meaningless, embarrassing, and intimate knot of our human birth. How true or defensive that derisive name is, what it captures or loses, are questions that the novel keeps always in play.

Roth's Pipik—who claims to be a former private detective from the Midwest, specializing in missing persons cases—has a grander view of his purpose. He is caught by the mad desire to become not so much Roth the novelist, the writer whose comic energies had so liberated him, as Roth's rejected public conscience, taking on a responsibility that he believes Roth himself has always evaded. This task includes his becoming the living archive of all of the abuse and bad reviews that have dogged Philip Roth throughout his career, but that he has rarely answered directly. Pipik is angered in particular about accusations that the novelist is an exposer of shameful Jewish secrets, a self-hating Jew, his own Shylock, since Pipik sees Roth as a great defender of Jewish history and consciousness. Listening to Pipik rehearse such old attacks, Roth feels as if a "genie of grievance had escaped the bottle in which a writer's resentments are pickled and preserved." The thorough lunacy, the desperate secondariness and parasitism of Pipik's existence are apparent even to Pipik himself. Yet still he demands, with a kind of wild bravado, that the real Philip Roth leave him alone to pursue his prophetic calling as the Theodor Herzl of Diasporism, and so stand as the public self, the salvific leader, the sacred king even, that Roth refuses to let himself become. "I AM YOUR GOOD NAME," Pipik writes in a desperate note he sends to Roth after they first meet, "THE NAKED YOU/THE MESSIANIC YOU/THE SACRIFICIAL YOU. . . . I AM THE YOU THAT IS NOT WORDS," he insists, claiming a debt and demanding a blessing from his author, demanding continued life as Philip Roth, with all the bitter eloquence of Victor Frankenstein's monster. It is a dream life in which resentment and redemption are inextricably bound up with each other.

Pathetic, fanatical, despairing, indeed sicker than the recovering Roth (he is dying of cancer), Pipik cannot simply be dismissed. Humorless as he appears, he is filled with an inventiveness and an inadvertently satiric energy that challenge the author's idea of himself, even as he reveals a history of weakness and self-loathing that Roth finds both alien and fascinating. Pipik is too concretely drawn in his gestures, his voice, even his stilted prose, for us to interpret him as a mere hallucination of the narrator. He is no dream, Roth insists, "however weightless and incorporeal life happens to feel at this moment and however alarmingly I may sense myself as a speck of being embodying nothing more than its own speckness, a tiny existence even more repugnant than his." Yet at the same time, Pipik is too outrageous to be other than a pure creature of the imagination, desperately trying to substantiate his nonentity. His ambiguity harrows Roth. "Is this a brilliant creative disposition whose ersatz satire I'm confronting, or a genuine ersatz maniac? . . . Suppose this Pipik of mine is none other than the Satiric Spirit in the flesh, and the whole thing a send-up, a satire of authorship," Dostoyevsky joining forces with Kafka and Aristophanes. This creature is, for Roth, as "hollow as Mortimer Snerd" (referring to the oafish sidekick of the clever Charlie McCarthy, both characters invented by the ventriloquist Edgar Bergen). Yet Pipik in the very energy of his negation possesses Roth, threatening to become the measure of all other fraudulence in the world.

In the maddest portions of the book, Roth tells of how he is drawn to take over the guise of his mocker. He seeks to out-Pipik Pipik in his ambitions as redeemer and curer of Jewish and anti-Jewish ills, as if he could consume the fantasy through its own excess. The game drives Roth's own dramatic and satiric inventiveness; it sustains his sense of writerly fortitude, his shameless and sometimes shameful need "to make the objective subjective and the subjective objective." He parodies his double even as he pursues him. Mistaken for Pipik wherever he goes, Roth takes over the sponsorship of Diasporism, stealing Pipik's harangues, his messianic ambitions, his prophetic rage, and mad theories. To take just one example among many, he dilates on the ways that Diasporism and its defense against Christian antisemitism is prefigured in the work of Irving Berlin, "the greatest Diasporist of all," who in his "Easter Parade" and "White Christmas" strips Christianity of its mythology of sacrifice and "*turns their religion into schlock*. But nicely! Nicely! So nicely the goyim don't even know what hit 'em. They love it." Laughing at Pipik is inevitable, but it is also dangerous. Roth's contempt for his double indeed releases in him a kind of chaos—or, perhaps, Pipik is that chaos. And Pipik himself cannot help but see in Roth, "laughing at him uncontrollably from behind the mask of his very own face, his worst enemy, the one to whom the only bond is hatred." The writer is drawn into Pipik's lunatic plots almost against his will—as when he tries to thwart the impostor's plan to kidnap Demjanjuk's son (with the help of Rabbi Meir Kahane) in order to compel the father to confess. Torn by desire and shame as much as fear and loathing, Roth finds that the pursuit of Pipik is endless; he is a wound that cannot be closed off. By the end of the novel Roth's life as much as his sanity seems in danger, and his very desire to save others from the rage that his contempt for

Pipik has unleashed becomes more and more grotesque, comically self-deceptive. That rage contaminates all sympathy. It also puts him at the mercy of the plots and paranoia of others. Every attempt to set things right, even to measure the scope of their wrongness, proves to be wrong. "Whatever I thought or did was wrong and for the simple reason that there was, I now realized, no *right thing* for someone whose double in this world was Mr. Moishe Pipik—so long as he and I both lived, this mental chaos would prevail. I'll never again know what's really going on or whether my thoughts are nonsense or not. . . . Even worse than never being free of him, I'll never again be free of myself; and nobody can know any better than I do that this is a punishment without limits. Pipik will follow me all the days of my life, and I will dwell in the house of Ambiguity forever." The parody of the Twenty-third Psalm invests Pipik with the power of an ironic blessing as much as a curse. One might think that Roth's book aims at an exorcism of Pipik, the mirror of the author's own uncertainty, just as *The Merchant of Venice* offers to exorcise Shylock. Yet the measure of the novel's success, like that of the play, lies in its failure to complete that exorcism. Roth's task is rather that of "exorcising and possessing him all at once." But this is a task without any obvious resolution, and when Pipik disappears from the novel toward its end one feels a loss or void in the narrator himself. He cannot, he tells us, even trust his power to imagine a proper death for such a creature as Pipik, however painful or outrageous that death might be. To frame such a death "wouldn't convince me of anything other than the power over my own imagination of that altogether human desire to be convinced by lies." Roth can never quite say of Pipik, "This thing of darkness I must acknowledge mine," though at one late, desolate moment, when he supposes himself to be Pipik's prisoner, he tries to appease his (absent) double with the words "I am Philip Roth and you are Philip Roth."

The struggle with Pipik, solipsistic as it may seem, occasions the emergence of other extreme, dangerous, and ambiguously imagined voices. Pipik's madness is a magnet for the madness of others.

These voices in turn reflect back on the complexities of Shylock's voice. Early in the novel, for example, we hear pieces of an interior monologue that the narrator attributes to John Demjanjuk as he sits placidly in the Jerusalem courtroom under Roth's gaze. Roth imagines Demjanjuk remembering in secret the truth of his violence during the war, the very thing that the court most wants to know but cannot confirm. It begins as a frightening kind job report:

Vigorous, healthy boy. Good worker. Never sick. Not even drink slowed him down. Just the opposite. Bludgeoned the bastards with an iron pipe, tore open the pregnant women with his sword, gouged out their eyes, whipped their flesh, drove nails through their ears, once took a drill and bored a hole right through someone's buttocks—felt like it that day, so he did it. . . . What a time! Nothing like it ever again! A mere twenty-two and he owned the place—could do to any of them whatever he wished . . . *boundlessly* powerful, like a god! Nearly a million of them, a *million*, and on every one a Jewish face in which he could read the terror. Of him. *Of him!* . . . One continuous party! Blood! Vodka! Women! Death! Power! And the screams! Those unending screams. And all of it *work*, good, hard work and yet wild, wild, untainted joy—the joy most people only get to dream of, nothing short of ecstasy!

This is not the banality of evil, but its frightening pleasure and mask of gleeful innocence. Here we get Roth at his most inventively unsettling, risking identification with the obscene, keeping the narrator himself implicated in the defendant's awful past (a past that might in this particular case, he admits, be an imagined thing, and Demjanjuk himself the victim of false accusation, since some evidence—even the weird texture of Demjanjuk's lies—points to his not being Ivan). There is no species of monster talk with which we or Roth have nothing to do. If you want to see what is at stake for a Renaissance author to grant humanity to a Jewish moneylender, he seems to say, you must also consider something like this.

Then there is the voice of an old friend Roth encounters in the

streets of Jerusalem, a Palestinian named George Ziad whom Roth
had known in his years as a graduate student at the University of
Chicago. The once witty, elegant youth is now almost unrecogniz-
able in the bitter survivor of twenty years of Israeli occupation. In
a remarkable piece of dramatic ventriloquism, Ziad—who thinks
that Roth is indeed the prophet of Diasporism—shares with his
friend his own half-demented theories about the violence of the
Israeli state and people. Early support for the existence of Israel
among Jews living in both America and Palestine, he argues, was
fed in part by a sense of shock at the destruction of European Jewry
and a desire to provide a refuge for those who survived, but also,
more darkly, by a hidden guilt, a suspicion that in their own calculated amnesia about if not outright contempt for the Jews of
Europe they had somehow "ignited" the Holocaust; they fear that
the catastrophe had been to some degree "instigated by the wish
to put an end to Jewish life in Europe that their massive emigration
had embodied, as though between the bestial destructiveness of
Hitlerian anti-Semitism and their own passionate desire to be deliv-
ered from the humiliations of their European imprisonment there
had existed some horrible, unthinkable interrelationship, bordering
on complicity." Warped by guilt and "undivulgable self-contempt,"
the Jews of Israel have hence abandoned the style of the Jew of
Europe, neurotic, alienated, self-questioning, yet "human, elastic,
adaptable, humorous, creative." In its place is a fixed mask of ideological certainty, an almost religious conviction that "Jews were
victims before they were conquerors and that they are conquerors
only because they are victims." In a terrible irony, the violence
against Palestinians which makes the Jews of Israel the doubles of
their own destroyers is sustained by a cynical manipulation of the
memory of the Shoah; Auschwitz justifies it all, and Israel draws
its legitimacy, its increasingly exhausted moral credit, "out of the
bank of the dead six million." The Demjanjuk trial is thus, for Ziad,
merely a show trial "to reinforce the cornerstone of Israeli power
politics by bolstering the ideology of the victim."

The empty puppet of his own hatred, Ziad appears to Roth as "someone aroused and decomposing all at the same time . . . as out of his depth as he was out of control," his words being "the shrewd and vacuous diatribe" of a man whose brain had been corroded by rage, to the point where his ideas acquire a fanatic intensity such that they scarcely seem like human thought. "At the core of everything was hatred and the great disabling fantasy of revenge." Ziad's words, like those lent to Demjanjuk, test our sympathy with the voice of resentment and with the theorizings of resentment, its endless creation of mirrors of itself. Elsewhere in the novel Roth offers his version of what John Keats called Shakespeare's "negative capability," that ability to be caught among doubts and mysteries without any nervous groping after certainties: "Better for real things to be uncontrollable, better for one's life to be indecipherable and intellectually impenetrable than to attempt to make causal sense of what is unknown with a fantasy that is mad." Such madness includes the utopian project of Pipik and the paranoid theories of Ziad; it speaks to the sources of antisemitism, with its mad making sense of a senseless world, its search for secret orders of mastery and cruelty.

Other characters add to the chorus of wounded, raging voices in the book, voices keyed to strange histories of survival. There is the terrified Apter, full of stories of those who "steal from him, spit at him, defraud and insult and humiliate him virtually every day," the largest number of these being survivors of the camps. There is a redheaded Ukranian Jewish giant—a golem, Roth imagines—who brokenly denounces an American Ukranian Orthodox priest who is preaching to the Jews in the streets of Jerusalem, trying to prevent them from martyring another innocent Christian, John Demjanjuk. Most central, however, is Pipik's lover and nurse, a Polish-American woman of fantastic healthiness named Wanda June, or Jinx, Possesski. Her story and her relation with Roth himself, one of seduction and betrayal, are as crucial as Pipik's. She is a "woman forged by the commonplace at its most cruelly ridiculous," hating both her treacherous former lovers and those religious sects, Protestant and Catholic, from whom she sought and failed to find a place of refuge. Having been turned into a "death-poisoned Jew-hating oncology nurse" working among Jewish doctors in a cancer ward, Jinx is bound to Pipik not only through love and pity but as a beneficiary of his other redemptive project, Anti-Semites Anonymous, an inner therapy to match the outward historical cure of Diasporism.

A commentary on this chaos of voices is provided by another survivor, an old man named Smilesburger, who accosts Roth in a Jerusalem restaurant, bearing himself toward the table on crutches, moving with a tortured ferocity. Roth describes him as "a mosaic of smithereens, cemented, sutured, wired, bolted," a human being whose bald, scaling, and furrowed head speaks for a mysterious power of continuity. Smilesburger tells Roth first that he is a wealthy American jeweler who has retired to Israel and gives him a million-dollar check in support of the Diasporist cause. As it turns out, he is a spy, or rather a spymaster, an upper-level operative in the Mossad, the Israeli secret service. Roth has been contacted to help them on a mission. Smilesburger knows that George Ziad, himself a Palestinian agent, had after his harangue against Israel asked his old friend Roth to fly in secret to Athens. There he is supposed to meet with the exiled Yasir Arafat and to speak at the same time with a cadre of American Jews who, in an awful extension of the Jewish appetite for justice, are funding Palestinian terrorism, even keeping the PLO's accounts. Smilesburger asks Roth to be a double agent, to go to Athens as Ziad wishes, but to report back to the Mossad, not so much about the PLO as about its Jewish supporters—a group that Smilesburger himself only half believes in, wondering whether it is not just a hallucination of Israeli paranoia. (The code name for the mission will be "Operation Shylock"; the password is "Three thousand ducats.") Smilesburger shares with Pipik and Ziad a desire to put Roth to use. Each wants to appropriate, even redeem, the fiction writer's fame and skill in impersonation for more worldly purposes, instrumentalizing the secret complicities of Roth's art, his stranger tradecraft. And like so many in this book, Smilesburger is a scholar of hatred, which for him includes the extravagances of Jewish hatred against other Jews. In order to win Roth's sympathy for the operation, and to get him to understand the origin of Jewish support for the PLO, Smilesburger delivers another of the novel's great arias, an account of the besetting Jewish obsession with *loshon hora*, the evil tongue. If this is something by which Jews have been most cruelly victimized, it is also something, he claims, for which Jews themselves have a peculiar genius. What draws his laments is indeed the *loshon hora* of Jews against Jews. Provoked originally by the continual inward and outward pressure of living in the midst of European antisemitism, Jewish *loshon hora* has yet acquired a fantastic life of its own. Hence the continual presence among Jews of "angry disputes, verbal abuse, malicious backbiting, mocking gossip, scoffing, faultfinding, complaining, condemning, insulting." It proliferates most in the very place where Jews should be free of fear, in the state of Israel. "The divisiveness is not just between Jew and Jew—it is within the individual Jew. . . . Inside every Jew there is a *mob* of Jews," all in endless dispute with one another. The flood of abuse can only be cured by the most rigorous charity, of the sort that is recommended by Smilesburger's idol, the rabbi Chofetz Chaim, who denounced even *loshon hora* spoken against oneself. Roth himself wonders if this sermon by Smilesburger is not just another subterfuge, a sly seduction. And the novel as a whole might suggest that the silencing of the evil tongue can only be a subtler lie, an evasion of the truths of human rage, whether rage against oneself or against others. For the book over its mad course speaks exactly to the revelatory energy of *loshon hora*, even its charity, its ruth as well as its wrath. Here, too, we may think of Shylock's dark pleasure, his way of turning his rage against his enemies even as he feeds on their hatred of him, facing them with an uncertain reflection of themselves.

Operation Shylock stands in the shadow of a history that

Shakespeare did not know and that even he could scarcely have imagined. Yet Roth's book tries to suggest just how *The Merchant of Venice* may help us take stock of that history and its aftermath. Roth reminds us of the complexity of such rage as Shylock's, the need to listen to it carefully; he shows a great trust in what Shakespeare made out of his own ignorant materials and what is laid bare in his fictive Jew—not just Shylock's status as an abused human being, but also his anger and impenetrability, his powers of improvisation, his willingness to "offend himself being offended." Shylock the clown and Shylock the king, even Shylock the false messiah, get shadowed in Roth's novel. It speaks of the place of the imaginary Jew within the lives of both Jews and non-Jews. The book also shows us something about the anarchic life that an author may grant to his literary doubles, even against his will or knowledge. It suggests the costs of this life. At one level, *Operation Shylock* tells the story of the ailing Roth's recovering the human strength he finds in fiction, even as he confronts in Pipik the self-wounding and self-dramatizing mirrors that feed his writing. To that degree it is about Roth's wrestling match in his fiction with both the real and the imaginary. This struggle includes Roth's wrestling match with Shakespeare, whose *Merchant of Venice* we are asked, in turn, to think of as a kind of "Operation Shylock," a cunning, risky cover for Shakespeare's own situation as a dramatist.

Within the blank spaces of Roth's novel one can feel something that brings into clearer view the blank spaces of the play. A friend once asked me how we might imagine Shylock's laughter after the trial. *Operation Shylock* helps us to imagine that laughter. One feels within its pages an abyss of laughter, a laughter emerging from the uncertain places within the real and within the self that such fictions can open up. (The laughter includes Demjanjuk's abysmal laughter during the trial at the confusion of a survivor who testifies against him.) We have a sense of a historical chaos driven by particular human appetites in all their rawness, driven by the will to play, by the love of theory itself, by the very energies that seek to order that chaos. Reading the book, one feels a Shakespearean ambition in Roth's inventions of voice, in his tragicomic generosity toward the obsessions of his characters, and in the way these obsessions reflect one another. We catch something of Shakespeare's attachment to characters who are radically unpredictable, at once overwhelmed and masterful, at the mercy not of some external fate but of the tricks played by their own imaginations, imaginations that yet participate in "the uncontrollability of real things." We see an image of human selves made monstrous by their own fears and desires, yet lent by those fears and desires their very humanity. And Roth, like Shakespeare, poses the question of how we are bound to the dangerous things that we ourselves have created or to which we have lent substance, things that can become "too dear for our possessing." *Operation Shylock* shares with *The Merchant of Venice* an interest in the aesthetics of repugnancy, a willingness to test the limits of the hateful and of hatred, the power of wounded voices—the source of his fascination, Roth acknowledges, with the bluntly, carelessly antisemitic writings of Louis-Ferdinand Céline. What Northrop Frye hears in Shylock, the voice of a mad-eyed loon standing outside the wedding feast, driven to speak obsessively of another world of suffering, marks part of Roth's ambition as well. Nothing human is alien to me.

Roth cannot command an audience whose members would take an antisemitic grotesque for granted, or an audience for whom Jews are entirely creatures of fiction. The blank spaces of Shakespeare's play are more chilling, its sympathies as well as its terrors are more mysterious, especially because the eruption of mystery centers so much around the single character of Shylock. There is in *Operation Shylock* no such solitude as that of Shakespeare's Jew, no loss or mourning like his, or any madness so lucid, notwithstanding all the domains of lucid madness that Roth lets us explore. Nor is there a character who seems so openly and unapologetically radiant with menace, whether in his willingness to terrify a court with the consequences of its own law or in his refusal to answer questions about the reasons for his viciousness. (Demjanjuk in his reverie at the trial comes closest, perhaps, but this is something only we hear.) The fright of Shylock's refusal to answer is hard to match in Roth, as is the demanding, harrowing silence built into his words; such silence is part of what makes his disappearance from the world of the play feel like a judgment upon that world, as no one is left to witness what cannot be spoken. The disappearance of Pipik is primarily a judgment upon Roth alone.

If we compare the novelist with the playwright, we may feel that Roth's mode of anarchic confession and his naked appetite for fictionalizing his life and literary reputation put his work as far as possible from the Shakespearean impersonality. Shylock in *The Merchant of Venice* can never know he is the double of his author, nor can Shakespeare confront his double within his own play. Roth in his novel can never shed his name, even if he contemplates its theft by another. Yet in the end Roth makes such differences part of his subject; he keeps faith with Shakespeare by his audacity rather than by his humility. If one can understand how Shakespeare found in Shylock a double, a means to articulate his doubt, desire, and rage, his troubled solitude as author, his wish to put his audience in its place, one feels more strongly the novel's ability to make us take up the play again. The desire to make something of Shylock survive the play, to make it stay in the world and become an inheritance for later watchers, is as strong in Roth's fiction as in those of Heine or Lewisohn. But his sense of what lives after the play is stranger. Shylock and Roth are both caught by an inheritance of blank, wounded need that the novelist will elsewhere call "the human stain," one face of which, for Roth, is Shylock himself. Another is the creature he calls Moishe Pipik. The question is how such an inheritance shapes what we know and our sense of what is possible. One name for that work is "Operation Shylock."

Dear Philip,
I went to the house. It's larger than I remembered and falling into ruin, the

stones are cracked, weeds spreading all over the yard, broken windows gaping. Someone had chalked on the front door the word "collaborator." I heard the noise of crows. People had been living there.

We should talk soon. There's something that I need to tell you about Shylock, I remembered it on the trip home. I've never told anyone. Let me know when and where we can meet.

Notes

PREFACE

Page viii

* Compact yet explosive: G. Wilson Knight, *Shakespearian Production, with Especial Reference to the Tragedies* (London: Routledge and Kegan Paul, 1964), 197.

Page ix

* "Tasted blood": John Berryman, *Berryman's Shakespeare: Essays, Letters, and Other Writings*, ed. John Haffenden (New York: Farrar, Straus and Giroux, 1999), 64.
* Shylock's "legacy": John Gross, *Shylock: A Legend and Its Legacy* (New York: Simon and Schuster, 1992). I am indebted to Gross's moving and scrupulous study throughout this book.

CHAPTER I: BEGINNING

Page 2

* "The accomplishment of an extremist": Wallace Stevens, "The Auroras of Autumn," in *The Palm at the End of the Mind: Selected Poems and a Play*, ed. Holly Stevens (New York: Alfred A. Knopf, 1971), 308.
* "Impenetrable, dark groundwork": William Hazlitt, *Hazlitt on Theatre*, ed. William Archer and Robert Lowe (New York: Hill and Wang, n.d.), 2.

Page 4

* Humanized the role: W. H. Auden, "Brothers and Others," in *The Dyer's Hand and Other Essays* (New York: Vintage Books, 1968), 223.

* "Part of the universal structure": Knight, *Shakespearian Production*, 196.

Page 5

* "An eloquence of being"; Angus Fletcher, conversation with the author.

* "It is often in his relative failures": R. P. Blackmur, *Studies in Henry James*, ed. Veronica A. Makowsky (New York: New Directions, 1983), 110.

Page 6

* "The figure of *the hated man*": Abraham Morevski, *Shylock and Shakespeare*, trans. Mirra Ginsburg (St. Louis: Fireside Books, 1967), 47.

Page 7

* "Scarcely more visible": Marcel Proust, *Time Regained*, vol. 6 of *In Search of Lost Time*, trans. Andreas Mayor and Terence Kilmartin, revised by D. J. Enright, 6 vols. (New York: Modern Library, 1993), 384.

* "What did this profit him?": Proust, *Time Regained*, 406.

Page 9

* Modernist images of the Jew: Richard Halpern, *Shakespeare among the Moderns* (Ithaca: Cornell University Press, 1997), 159–226.

Page 10

* Taking to one's bed: Franz Kakfa, "The Hunter Gracchus," in *The Complete Stories*, ed. Nahum N. Glatzer (New York: Schocken, 1971), 230.

Page 11

* "The seed of a possible hell": Jorge Luis Borges, "*Deutsches Requiem*," in *Collected Fictions*, trans. Andrew Hurley (Harmondsworth: Penguin Books, 1998), 232.

Page 12

* "A sixteenth-century London moneylender tries in vain": Borges, "*Deutsches Requiem*," 232.

* "The historian, essentially, wants more documents": Henry James, preface to *The Aspern Papers, The Turn of the Screw, The Liar, The Two Faces*, vol. 12 of *The New York Edition of the Novels and Tales of Henry James*, 26 vols. (New York: Scribner's, 1908), vii.

CHAPTER 2: THE HEART OF IT

Page 14

∗ The name Shylock itself is . . . no invention: Stephen Orgel, *Imagining Shakespeare: A History of Texts and Visions* (Houndmills: Palgrave Macmillan, 2003), 151–52.

Page 15

∗ *Professional gamblers*: Cf. Kenneth Burke, "Antony in Behalf of the Play," in *The Philosophy of Literary Form: Studies in Symbolic Action*, 3rd ed. (Berkeley: University of California Press, 1973), 336.

CHAPTER 3: SHYLOCK'S NOTHING

Page 22

∗ "Synonymous with kept": Robert Frost, "The Constant Symbol," in *Robert Frost: Collected Poems, Prose, and Plays* (New York: Library of America, 1995), 786.

∗ Shakespeare's "spectral generosity": William Flesch, *Generosity and the Limits of Authority: Shakespeare, Herbert, Milton* (Ithaca: Cornell University Press, 1992), 147–88.

∗ His own poetic powers: W. H. Auden, *Lectures on Shakespeare*, ed. Arthur Kirsch (Princeton: Princeton University Press, 2000), 97–98.

Page 23

∗ Map, prayer, or dream: Burke, *The Philosophy of Literary Form*, 5–7.

Page 26

∗ "Commodity and gift": Anne Carson, *Economy of the Unlost (Reading Simonides of Keos with Paul Celan)* (Princeton: Princeton University Press, 1999), 43.

∗ "A guarantee of exchange": Aristotle, *Nichomachean Ethics* 1133b11–13, quoted in Carson, *Economy of the Unlost*, 78.

Page 27

∗ "Provoked by a perception of absence": Carson, *Economy of the Unlost*, 108, 59.

CHAPTER 4: THE HOUSE OF THE THREE CASKETS

Page 30

* The maximum amount of magic: William Empson, *Some Versions of Pastoral* (New York: New Directions, 1974), 29–30, 27–88 more generally.

Page 31

* "Things unforgotten, unshriven, unexpurgated": F. Scott Fitzgerald, *Tender Is the Night* (New York: Scribner's, 1996), 101.

* "The strongest guard": Fitzgerald, *Tender Is the Night*, 80.

* Gold as a soul symbol: Knight, *Shakespearian Production*, 190, 198.

Page 34

* "Part of nature and therefore subject": Sigmund Freud, "The Theme of the Three Caskets," in *Collected Papers*, ed. Joan Riviere, 5 vols. (London: Hogarth Press, 1946), 4:253.

* Freud's essay curiously evades or occludes: Marjorie Garber, *Shakespeare's Ghost Writers: Literature as Uncanny Causality* (New York: Methuen, 1987), 74–86.

* Portia a fairy-tale princess: Theodor Reik, *The Secret Self: Psychoanalytic Experiences in Life and Literature* (New York: Grove Press, 1952), 77–96.

Page 35

* The enchantress Medea: Leslie A. Fiedler, *The Stranger in Shakespeare* (New York: Stein and Day, 1972), 112–13.

Page 37

* The mysterious logic of exchange: Marc Shell, *Money, Language, and Thought: Literary and Philosophical Economies from the Medieval to the Modern Era* (Berkeley: University of California Press, 1982), 47–83.

Page 42

* The idea of private property: Kenneth Burke, "Othello: An Essay to Illustrate a Method," in *Perspectives by Incongruity* , ed. Stanley Edgar Hyman (Bloomington: Indiana University Press, 1964), 190.

CHAPTER 5: EXCHANGES

Page 44

* "Puts to moral death the words": Philip Brockbank, *On Shakespeare: Jesus, Shakespeare and Karl Marx, and Other Essays* (Oxford: Blackwell, 1989), 12.

Page 45

* A kind of infection: Thomas Wilson, *A Discourse upon Usury* (1572), ed. R. H. Tawney (New York: Harcourt, Brace, and Co., 1925), especially 213–33, 252–73.

* "Brothers" have become potential "others": See Benjamin N. Nelson, *The Idea of Usury: From Tribal Brotherhood to Universal Otherhood* (Princeton: Princeton University Press, 1949).

Page 46

* Man's dependence on the world: Auden, *The Dyer's Hand*, 234–35.

Page 47

* An emblem of "Occasion": Geffrey Whitney, *A Choice of Emblemes and Other Devises* (Leyden, 1586), 181.

Page 48

* Antonio's melancholy: Harold C. Goddard, *The Meaning of Shakespeare* (Chicago: University of Chicago Press, 1951), 81–116.

* "A psychopath of the business world": Angus Fletcher, letter to the author.

Page 49

* His unacknowledged double: Goddard, *The Meaning of Shakespeare*, 92; René Girard, "'To entrap the wisest': A Reading of *The Merchant of Venice*," in *Literature and Society: Selected Papers from the English Institute*, ed. Edward Said (New York: Columbia University Press, 1980), 100–119.

Page 50

* More to inward conscience than to outward law: See Norman Jones, *God and the Moneylenders: Usury and Law in Early Modern England* (Oxford: Blackwell, 1989), 145–74.

* "We need not wonder why so often": Harold Fisch, *Hamlet and the Word: The Covenant Pattern in Shakespeare* (New York: Ungar, 1971), 114.

Page 51

* "Between shadowy symbols and substantial things": Shell, *Money, Language, and Thought*, 185.

Page 52

* "That the Jew is strained to become a merciful Christian": Shell, *Money, Language, and Thought*, 74.

CHAPTER 6: SHYLOCK UNBOUND

Page 55

* His peculiar idiom or dramatic idiolect: Otto Jespersen, *Growth and Structure of the English Language* (New York: Anchor, 1956), 232–34.

Page 56

* The accountant's manner: Gross, *Shylock*, 66.

Page 57

* "What would be missing": Ludwig Wittgenstein, *Philosophical Investigations*, trans. G. E. M. Anscombe (New York: Macmillan, 1953), 214e.

Page 61

* "Is not to get behind and justify itself": Charles Spinosa, "Shylock and Debt and Contract in *The Merchant of Venice*," *Cardozo Studies in Law and Literature* 5, no. 1 (1993): 79.

Page 62

* "To explore and deepen": Spinosa, "Shylock and Debt and Contract," 75.

* The power *of* silence and the power *to* silence: See Paolo Valesio, *Ascoltare il silenzio: La retorica come teoria* (Bologna: Il Mulino, 1986), 341–426.

* Aeschylus's Erinyes: Knight, *Shakespearian Production*, 192

Page 63

* "Simple repetition metamorphosing": R. P. Blackmur, *Language as Gesture: Essays in Poetry* (New York: Harcourt Brace Jovanovich, 1952), 13.

* "The resultant meaning": Blackmur, *Language as Gesture*, 13.

CHAPTER 7: ARE YOU ANSWERED?

Page 67

* "Straight from his own unconscious": Gross, *Shylock*, 83.

Page 68

* "I have seen some": Michel de Montaigne, "An Apologie for Raymond Sebond," in *Essays*, trans. John Florio, 3 vols. (London: J. M. Dent, 1910), 2:316.

* "I cruelly hate cruelty": Michel de Montaigne, "Of Cruelty," in *The Complete Essays*, trans. Donald M. Frame (Stanford: Stanford University Press, 1958), 313.

* "We must become like the animals": Montaigne, "Apology for Raymond Sebond," in *The Complete Essays*, 363.

* Not to sound crazy to himself: See Shoshana Felman, *The Juridical Unconscious: Trials and Traumas in the Twentieth Century* (Cambridge, MA: Harvard University Press, 2002), 125.

Page 70

* Influx of powerful doubts: Stanley Cavell, *The Claim of Reason: Wittgenstein, Skepticism, Morality, and Tragedy* (Oxford: Oxford University Press, 1979), 478–81.

* "May include repulsion or fear": P. F. Strawson, *Freedom and Resentment and Other Essays* (London: Methuen, 1974), 9.

* "Do not invite us to view": Strawson, *Freedom and Resentment*, 7.

Page 71

* "You cannot quarrel with him": Strawson, *Freedom and Resentment*, 9.

* "Thickly entangled forest": Strawson, *Freedom and Resentment*, 24.

Page 72

* The two words are indeed linked etymologically: See Eric Partridge, *Origins: A Short Etymological Dictionary of Modern English* (London: Routledge and Kegan Paul, 1958), s.v. "market" (p. 382).

* "In general, though within varying limits": Strawson, *Freedom and Resentment*, 15–16.

Page 74

* A monstrous, tusked sow: See Isaiah Shachar, *The "Judensau": A*

Page 74 (continued)

Medieval Anti-Jewish Motif and Its History, Warburg Institute Surveys, no. 5 (London: Warburg Institute, 1974).

* "It would be to lay too limited an emphasis": Knight, *Shakespearian Production*, 198.

CHAPTER 8: A THEATER OF COMPLICITY

Page 75

* "An actor's actor": Lawrence Danson, *The Harmonies of "The Merchant of Venice"* (New Haven: Yale University Press, 1978), 154.

Page 79

* "Pulcinella, in desperate need": Mel Gordon, *Lazzi: The Comic Routines of the Commedia dell'Arte* (New York: Performing Journal Publications, 1983), 18. The clown named Cola can replace Pulcinella in this scene, Gordon indicates.

* "Comparative hardness of heart": Elmer Edgar Stoll, *Shakespeare Studies, Historical and Comparative in Method* (New York: Macmillan, 1927), 308.

* "Passes over the border": Stoll, *Shakespeare Studies*, 314.

* Sentimentality about victims: C. L. Barber, *Shakespeare's Festive Comedy: A Study of Dramatic Form and Its Relation to Social Context* (Princeton: Princeton University Press, 1959), 163–91.

* "Control our own fears": Judith Shklar, *Ordinary Vices* (Cambridge, MA: Harvard University Press, 1984), 17.

Page 80

* The way of all clowns: Walter Kerr, *Tragedy and Comedy* (New York: Simon and Schuster, 1967), 19–35.

* "What fascinates us about the *idiotes*": Northrop Frye, *A Natural Perspective: The Development of Shakespearean Comedy and Romance* (New York: Columbia University Press, 1965), 101.

Page 82

* Shylock is no monster: Arnold Wesker, *The Birth of Shylock and the Death of Zero Mostel* (New York: Fromm International, 1999).

* Roles written for the stage: Michael Goldman, *The Actor's Freedom: Toward a Theory of Drama* (New York: Viking, 1975), 53–110.

CHAPTER 9: THE THIRD POSSESSOR

Page 85

* A daimonic or allegorical agent: Angus Fletcher, *Allegory: The Theory of a Symbolic Mode* (Ithaca: Cornell University Press, 1964), 25–69.

Page 86

* Mocks by literalization: See James Shapiro, Shakespeare and the Jews (New York: Columbia University Press, 1996), 113–30.

* More theological readings: Danson, *Harmonies*; Anthony Hecht, "*The Merchant of Venice*: A Venture in Hermeneutics," in *Obbligati: Essays in Criticism* (New York: Atheneum, 1986), 140–229; and Barbara K. Lewalski, "Biblical Allusion and Allegory in *The Merchant of Venice*," *Shakespeare Quarterly* 13 (1962): 327–43.

* An equivocal threshold: see Julia Reinhard Lupton, *Citizen-Saints: Shakespeare and Political Theology* (Chicago: University of Chicago Press, 2005).

Page 87

* To give a more local grounding: M. M. Mahood, appendix to her edition of *The Merchant of Venice* (Cambridge: Cambridge University Press, 1987), 184–88.

Page 89

* Rebekah's "courageous" lie: Martin Luther, *Lectures on Genesis, Chapters 26–30*, vol. 5 of *Luther's Works*, ed. Jaroslav Pelikan, 55 vols. (St. Louis: Concordia Publishing House, 1955–68), 111.

* Like Calvin: John Calvin, *Genesis*, ed. Alister McGrath and J. I. Packer (Wheaton, IL: Crossway Books, 2001), 235–45.

* A type of usurious greed: Joan Ozark Holmer, *The Merchant of Venice: Choice, Hazard and Consequence* (New York: St. Martin's Press, 1995), 157–60. See also Luther, *Lectures on Genesis*, 375–78.

Page 90

* A fearful symbol: See Hyam Maccoby, *The Sacred Executioner: Human Sacrifice and the Legacy of Guilt* (London: Thames and Hudson, 1982);

Page 90 (continued)

Jon D. Levenson, *The Death and Resurrection of the Beloved Son: The Transformation of Child Sacrifice in Judaism and Christianity* (New Haven: Yale University Press, 1993), 111–42; and Fiedler, *The Stranger in Shakespeare*, 124–25.

Page 91

* Old Jacob himself tricked: Douglas Anderson, "The Old Testament Presence in *The Merchant of Venice*," *ELH* 52, no. 1 (1985): 120.

* Revival of the study of Hebrew: See Jerome Friedman, *The Most Ancient Testimony: Sixteenth-Century Christian-Hebraica in the Age of Renaissance Nostalgia* (Athens: Ohio University Press, 1983); G. Lloyd Jones, *The Discovery of Hebrew in Tudor England: A Third Language* (Manchester: Manchester University Press, 1983).

Page 92

* Mirrored their own concerns: See Arnold Williams, *The Common Expositor: An Account of the Commentaries on Genesis, 1527–1633* (Chapel Hill: University of North Carolina Press, 1948), 172.

* Images of a spiritual life: James Samuel Preus, *From Shadow to Promise: Old Testament Interpretation from Augustine to the Young Luther* (Cambridge, MA: Harvard University Press, 1969), 200–65.

Page 92 (continued)

* "They wot not what more profit": William Tyndale, *Tyndale's Old Testament*, ed. David Daniell (New Haven: Yale University Press, 1992), 8.

Page 93

* "Candid realism": Geoffrey Hartman, *Scars of the Spirit: The Struggle against Inauthenticity* (New York: Palgrave Macmillan, 2002), 110, 116.

* Murder of an Egyptian: Tom Bishop, "Othello in the Wilderness" (unpublished essay).

Page 94

* The "theomorphic" aspects: Harold Bloom, *Ruin the Sacred Truths: Poetry and Belief from the Bible to the Present* (Cambridge, MA: Harvard University Press, 1989), 7.

* Refuge in the world of time: Theodor Reik, *The Search Within: The*

Inner Experiences of a Psychoanalyst (New York: Farrar, Straus and Cudahy, 1956), 360, 365–66; and Heinrich Heine, "The Gods in Exile," in *The Works of Heinrich Heine*, trans. Charles Godfrey Leland, 20 vols. (New York: Croscup and Sterling, n.d.), 12: 293–377.

* The mask of a Jewish cantor: Heinrich Heine, "The God Apollo" [Der Apollogott], in *The Complete Poems of Heinrich Heine*, trans. Hal Draper (Boston: Suhrkamp/Insel, 1982), 580–83.

* Impulses that have been abandoned or neglected: Roger F. Cook, *By the Rivers of Babylon: Heinrich Heine's Late Songs and Reflections* (Detroit: Wayne State University Press, 1998), 143–47.

Page 95

* Figure of Punch: Herbert Marks, conversation with the author.

Page 96

* Blessed by the example of Job's protests: Søren Kierkegaard, *Fear and Trembling/Repetition*, trans. Howard V. Hong and Edna H. Hong (Princeton: Princeton University Press, 1983), 198.

Page 100

* "Like the laws of Moses": Lisa Freinkel, *Reading Shakespeare's Will: The Theology of Figure from Augustine to the Sonnets* (New York: Columbia University Press, 2002), 289.

Page 101

* Secret "sowle and spyrit": Edward Hake, *Epieikeia: A Dialogue on Equity in Three Parts* (ca. 1601), ed. D. E. C. Yale (New Haven: Yale University Press, 1953), 28.

* "A situation where norms have disappeared": Theodore Ziolkowski, *The Mirror of Justice: Literary Reflections of Legal Crises* (Princeton: Princeton University Press, 1997), 172.

Page 103

* Their unacknowledged guilt: Harold Fisch, *The Dual Image: The Figure of the Jew in English and American Literature* (New York: Ktav Publishing, 1971), 22–23.

Page 104

* *Moves as I myself am moved*: Cf. Anthony Burgess, *Nothing like the Sun: A Story of Shakespeare's Love-Life* (New York: Norton, 1975), 123.

CHAPTER 10: CONVERSION

Page 107

* "Internalizing justice": Frye, *A Natural Perspective*, 102.
* Conversion of the Jews: Shapiro, *Shakespeare and the Jews*, 131–66.

Page 108

* "The Jew scanned his tormentor": Quoted in Laurence Irving, *Henry Irving: The Actor and His World* (London: Faber, 1951), 344.
* Doubling of his exile and his promised conversion: see Michael Ragussis, *Figures of Conversion: "The Jewish Question" and English National Identity* (Durham: Duke University Press, 1995), 76–79.

Pages 109–10

* Travelers' tales: See Peter Berek, "The Jew as Renaissance Man," *Renaissance Quarterly* 51, no. 1 (1998): 140–44.

Page 110

* "Cruell and barbarous Inquisition": John Foxe, *Actes and Monuments*, 4th ed., 8 vols., ed. Josiah Pratt (London, 1877), 4:451; quoted in Sharon Achinstein, "John Foxe and the Jews," *Renaissance Quarterly* 54, no. 1 (2001): 99.
* Church laws against forced conversion: See Solomon Grayzel, "The Papal Bull *Sicut Judeis*," in *Essential Papers on Judaism and Christianity in Conflict: From Late Antiquity to the Reformation*, ed. Jeremy Cohen (New York: New York University Press, 1991), 231–59.
* A sacrament that could not be annulled: Cecil Roth, *A History of the Marranos* (Philadelphia: Jewish Publication Society, 1932), 18–19.
* Spain in 1391: Ytzhak Baer, *A History of the Jews in Christian Spain*, trans. Louis Schoffman, 2 vols. (Philadelphia: Jewish Publication Society, 1961), 2:95–169; Salo Wittmayer Baron, *A Social and Religious History of the Jews*, 2nd rev. ed., 18 vols. (New York: Columbia University Press, 1952–83), 11:232–36.
* Tortosa disputation: Baer, *A History of the Jews in Christian Spain*, 2:170–243; Hyam Maccoby, ed. and trans., *Judaism on Trial: Jewish-Christian Disputations in the Middle Ages* (East Brunswick, NJ: Associated University Presses, 1982), 82–94, 168–215.

Page 111

* "Conversion by persuasion": Brian Pullan, *The Jews of Europe and the Inquisition of Venice, 1550–1670* (Totowa, NJ: Barnes and Noble Books, 1983), 246.

* "By ambition or despair, by prudence or cowardice": Léon Poliakov, *From Mohammed to the Marranos*, trans. Natalie Gerardi, vol. 2 of *The History of Anti-Semitism* (New York: Vanguard Press, 1973), 159.

* "A secret war": Poliakov, *From Mohammed to the Marranos*, 242.

* Sectarian hatred: Poliakov, *From Mohammed to the Marranos*, 181.

* Monster with "a wolf's mouth": Michael Alpert, *Crypto-Judaism and the Spanish Inquisition* (Houndsmills: Palgrave, 2001), 12.

* "Purity of blood": Poliakov, *From Mohammed to the Marranos*, 222–32.

Page 112

* "If any distinction at all was made": Poliakov, *From Mohammed to the Marranos*, 180.

* Fall out of affiliation: Benzion Netanyahu, *The Marranos of Spain from the Late XIVth to the Early XVIth Century, According to Contemporary Hebrew Sources* (New York: American Academy for Jewish Research, 1966).

* "Mockingly advised Old Christians": Baron, *A Social and Religious History of the Jews*, 13:68.

Page 113

* "An exposed and solitary consciousness": Stephen Gilman, *The Spain of Fernando de Rojas: The Intellectual and Social Landscape of* La Celestina (Princeton: Princeton University Press, 1972), 180.

* The humanist pedagogue Juan Luis Vives: See Américo Castro, *The Structure of Spanish History*, trans. Edmund L. King (Princeton: Princeton University Press, 1954), 577–84; and Carlos G. Noreña, *Juan Luis Vives* (The Hague: Nijhoff, 1970), 18–28.

* The anarchic intelligence of Fernando de Rojas: Gilman, *The Spain of Fernando de Rojas*, 111–267.

* Rojas's father and father-in-law condemned: Gilman, *The Spain of Fernando de Rojas*, 45, 65–110.

Page 113 (continued)

* Vives's parents condemned: Noreña, *Juan Luis Vives*, 20.

* Underwent repeated baptisms: Pullan, *The Jews of Europe*, 295.

Page 114

* Guides to help inquisitors: Norman Roth, *Conversos, Inquisition, and the Expulsion of the Jews from Spain* (Madison: University of Wisconsin Press, 1995), 189.

* Spanish word for swine: See Arturo Farinelli, *Marrano (Storia di un vituperio)* (Geneva: Olschki, 1925), 11–19.

Pages 114–15

* Shadowy, equivocal religious practices: Cecil Roth, "The Religion of the Marranos," *Jewish Quarterly Review*, n.s., 22 (1931): 1–35; David M. Gitlitz, *Secrecy and Deceit: The Religion of the Crypto-Jews* (Philadelphia: Jewish Publication Society, 1996).

Page 115

* "Inner psychological identification": Yosef Kaplan, "The Portugese Community of Amsterdam in the 17th Century between Tradition and Change," in *Society and Community: Proceedings of the Second International Congress for Research of the Sephardi and Oriental Jewish Heritage*, ed. Abraham Haim (Jerusalem: Misgav, 1984), 146; quoted in Gitlitz, *Secrecy and Deceit*, 46.

* "I lit the Sabbath candles": Gitlitz, *Secrecy and Deceit*, 83.

* The "romance" of the Marrano: Cecil Roth, *A History of the Marranos*, 28.

* "The marrano epic": Poliakov, *From Mohammed to the Marranos*, 233.

* "The cleavages in the marrano conscience": Carl Gebhardt, *Die Schriften des Uriel da Costa* (Amsterdam, 1922), xxiii, quoted in Poliakov, *From Mohammed to the Marranos*, 278.

* The person of Isaac Cardoso: Yosef Hayim Yerushalmi, *From Spanish Court to Italian Ghetto: Isaac Cardoso: A Study in Seventeenth-Century Marranism and Jewish Apologetics* (New York: Columbia University Press, 1971).

Page 116

* "He was solemnly expelled": Heinrich Heine, "Religion and

Philosophy in Germany," in *Selected Prose*, ed. and trans. Ritchie
Robertson (Harmondsworth: Penguin, 1993), 243.

Page 117

* "To save human beings": Gabriel Albiac, "The Empty Synagogue,"
  trans. Ted Stolze, in *The New Spinoza*, ed. Warren Montag and Ted
  Stolze, Theory out of Bounds, vol. 11 (Minneapolis: University of
  Minneapolis Press, 1997), 137. This piece is an excerpt from Albiac,
  La sinagoga vacía: Un estudo de las fuentes marranas del espinosismo
  (Madrid, 1987).

* "Marrano of reason": Yirmiyahu Yovel, *Spinoza and Other Heretics:
  The Marrano of Reason* (Princeton: Princeton University Press, 1989),
  15–39.

* Historical self-consciousness and spiritual vitality: Gershom
  Scholem, *The Messianic Idea in Judaism and Other Essays on Jewish
  Spirituality* (New York: Schocken, 1971), 78–141.

Page 118

* "From Marakesh to Vilno": Yovel, *Spinoza and Other Heretics*, 191.

* "Assume the form of evil": Gershom Scholem, *Sabbatai Ṣevi: The
  Mystical Messiah, 1626–1676*, trans. R. J. Zwiwerblowsky (Princeton:
  Princeton University Press, 1973), 801.

* "The Messiah must go his lonely way": Scholem, *The Messianic Idea*,
  108.

* "It is ordained that the King Messiah": Cardoso, quoted in Scholem,
  The Messianic Idea, 95.

* "The half-light of a faith": Scholem, *The Messianic Idea*, 141.

Page 119

* "Genuine desires for a reconsecration": Scholem, *The Messianic Idea*, 112

* "Necessary angel of earth": Stevens, "Angel Surrounded by Paysans,"
  in *The Palm at the End of the Mind*, 354.

* "A focus on the iconography of tradition": Robert Alter, *Necessary
  Angels: Tradition and Modernity in Kafka, Benjamin, and Scholem*
  (Cambridge, MA: Harvard University Press, 1991), 115.

Page 121

* "The impossibility of crows": Franz Kafka, *Dearest Father: Stories and*

Page 121 (continued)

> *Other Writings*, ed. Max Brod, trans. Ernst Kaiser and Eithne Wilkins
> (New York: Schocken, 1954), 37.

* "I think the key to Kafka's work": Walter Benjamin, letter to
  Gershom Scholem (4 February 1939), in *The Correspondence of Walter
  Benjamin and Gershom Scholem, 1932–1940*, ed. Gershom Scholem,
  trans. Gary Smith and Andre Lefevere (New York: Schocken, 1989),
  243 (emphasis in original).

* "The eternal questioning Satan": Frye, *A Natural Perspective*, 103–4.

Page 122

* The case of a woman: Described in N. Elena Vanzan Marchini, "Il
  dramma dei convertiti nella follia di una ex ebrea," *La Rassegna men-
  sile di Israel* (January–February 1980), 3–30; and Pullan, *The Jews of
  Europe*, 282–87. The full text of the testimony in the case is printed
  in Pier Cesare Ioly Zorattini, ed. *Processi del S. Uffizio di Venezia contro
  Ebrei e Giudaizzanti (1548–60)*, Storia dell'Ebraismo in Italia: Studi e
  Testi 2 (Florence: Leo S. Olschki, 1980), 151–224.

* "The bastard son of a whore": Ioly Zorattini, *Processi*, 152 (my translation).

* "Who is not a good Jew": Ioly Zorattini, *Processi*, 158 (my translation).

Page 123

* Disputes with persons in the empty air: Pullan, *The Jews of Europe*,
  286.

* And other nameless adversaries: Ioly Zorattini, *Processi*, 206.

* Christ she called: Ioly Zorattini, *Processi*, 156.

* "Bloodless phantasm of that tradition": Vanzan Marchini, "Il
  dramma dei convertiti," 30 (my translation).

CHAPTER II: GOLEMS AND GHOSTS

Page 124

* A life that continues beyond the confines of the play: Ludwig
  Lewisohn, *The Last Days of Shylock* (New York: Harper and Brothers,
  1931).

Page 125

* "Foul and arrogant superstition": Lewisohn, *The Last Days of Shylock*, 83.

Page 130

* "Keen eyeballs peered": Heinrich Heine, letter on Edmund Kean, trans. S. S. Prawer, in *Heine's Jewish Comedy* (Oxford: Oxford University Press, 1983), 275–76.

* "A pale British beauty": Heinrich Heine, *Shakespeare's Girls and Women*, in Prawer, *Heine's Jewish Comedy*, 292.

Page 131

* "The lower and the higher mob." Heine, *Shakespeare's Girls and Women*, 293.

* "The deep affinity": *The Poetry and Prose of Heinrich Heine*, ed. and trans. Frederic Ewen (New York: Citadel Press, 1948), 678.

* "Neither Jews nor Christians": *The Poetry and Prose of Heinrich Heine*, 672.

Page 132

* Probes his own wounds: Jeffrey L. Sammons, *Heinrich Heine: A Modern Biography* (Princeton: Princeton University Press, 1979), 110.

* "Chose the hard case": Gross, *Shylock*, 264.

* Baron James de Rothschild: Heine, *Shakespeare's Girls and Women*, 294.

* "The Jews happened just then": Heine, *Shakespeare's Girls and Women*, 294–95.

Page 134

* "If one day Satan": Heine, *Shakespeare's Girls and Women*, 295.

* "The most fruitful soil for pantheism": Heine, "Religion and Philosophy in Germany," 250.

* Lent their destructive power: Heine, "Religion and Philosophy in Germany," 248.

* A poem from 1844, commemorating the dedication: "The New Israelite Hospital in Hamburg," in *The Complete Poems of Heinrich Heine*, 398–99.

* "Though I looked all around in the synagogue": Heine, *Shakespeare's Girls and Women*, 296.

Page 135

* His early poem "Almansor": *The Complete Poems of Heinrich Heine*, 117–20.

* "Elegiac whining, humming": "Jehuda ben Halevy," in *The Complete Poems of Heinrich Heine*, 659.

Page 138

* "Loathsome Jewish swine": Ingmar Bergman, *Fanny and Alexander*, trans. Alan Blair (New York: Pantheon Books, 1982), 164.

Page 139

* "A horrible scream echoing": Bergman, *Fanny and Alexander*, 200.

CHAPTER 12: A DREAM

Page 140

* The orchestra of an old theater: See Franz Kafka, *Diaries, 1910–1913*, ed. Max Brod, trans. Joseph Kresh (New York: Schocken, 1948), 153–56 ("Dream: In the theater").

CHAPTER 13: ESTHÉTIQUE DU MAL

Page 143

* "The pool of indeterminacy": John Hollander, "The Problem of Shylock" (unpublished review of *Shylock: A Legend and Its Legacy*, by John Gross).

* "Evil-mindedness": Hans Jonas, "The Abyss of the Will: Philosophical Meditation on the Seventh Chapter of Paul's Epistle to the Romans," in *Philosophical Essays: From Ancient Creed to Technological Man* (Chicago: University of Chicago Press, 1974), 343.

Page 144

* Projects the unredeemed half: Rosemary Radford Ruether, *Faith and Fratricide: The Theological Roots of Anti-Semitism* (Minneapolis: Seabury Press, 1974), 131.

* A larger process of self-criticism: See Ruether, *Faith and Fratricide*, 137.

* Might serve to localize doubts: Gavin I. Langmuir, *Toward a Theory of Antisemitism* (Berkeley: University of California Press, 1990), 100–33.

Page 145

* "Charting evil's invasion": Heiko A. Oberman, *The Roots of Anti-Semitism in the Age of Renaissance and Reformation*, trans. James I. Porter (Philadelphia: Fortress Press, 1984), 105.

* Augustine's formula: Augustine, *In Ps. Enarr*, 1:21, quoted in Marcel Simon, "Christian Anti-Semitism," in Cohen, *Essential Papers on Judaism and Christianity in Conflict*, 161.

* Rationalizing projections: Max Horkheimer and Theodor W. Adorno, *Dialectic of Enlightenment: Philosophical Fragments*, ed. Gunzelin Schmid Noerr, trans. Edmund Jephcott (Stanford: Stanford University Press, 2002), 137–72.

* A person turned to stone: Jean-Paul Sartre, *Anti-Semite and Jew*, trans. George J. Becker (New York: Schocken, 1948), 18–54.

Page 146

* Lunatic logic: Hannah Arendt, *The Origins of Totalitarianism* (New York: Schocken, 2004), 3–155.

* The role of intransigent alien: Hannah Arendt, "The Jew as Pariah: A Hidden Tradition," in *The Jew as Pariah: Jewish Identity and Politics in the Modern Age*, ed. Ron H. Feldman (New York: Grove Press, 1978), 67–90.

* "The ways in which they saw and felt the world": George Kateb, *Hannah Arendt: Politics, Conscience, Evil* (Totawa, NJ: Rowman and Allanheld, 1984), 61.

Page 147

* No real interest in religion: George Santayana, *Interpretations of Poetry and Religion*, ed. William G. Holzberger and Herman J. Saatkamp, Jr. (Cambridge, MA: MIT Press, 1989), 91–103.

Page 149

* Refusal to take sides: Norman Rabkin, *Shakespeare and the Problem of Meaning* (Chicago: Chicago University Press, 1981), 1–32.

* The strong kid: Angus Fletcher, letter to the author.

Page 151

* Love that is blocked or misdirected: Oscar Pfister, *Christianity and Fear: A Study in History and in the Psychology and Hygiene of Religion*

Page 151 (continued)

(German original, 1944), trans. W. H. Johnston (New York: Macmillan, 1948).

* The small group of conversos: Lucien Wolf, "Jews in Elizabethan England," *Transactions of the Jewish Historical Society of England* 11 (1928): 1–91; David S. Katz, *The Jews in the History of England, 1485–1850* (Oxford: Oxford University Press, 1994), 15–106; and Shapiro, *Shakespeare and the Jews*, 62–76.

* Implicated in Anglo-Spanish espionage: Katz, *The Jews in the History of England*, 49–106.

Page 152

* Experience of secrecy and equivocation: See Perez Zagorin, *Ways of Lying: Dissimulation, Persecution, and Conformity in Early Modern Europe* (Cambridge, MA: Harvard University Press, 1990), 132–52

* Shadow of a religious mythology: Stephen Greenblatt, *Hamlet in Purgatory* (Princeton: Princeton University Press, 2001).

Page 155

* "The instant when a person becomes": Arendt, *The Origins of Totalitarianism*, 383.

* "The disturbing miracle": Arendt, *The Origins of Totalitarianism*, 382.

Page 156

* "The arbitrariness inherent in all beginnings": Hannah Arendt, *On Revolution* (New York: Viking, 1963), 210.

CHAPTER 14: OPERATION SHYLOCK

Page 158

* "The savage, repellent, and villainous Jew": Philip Roth, *Operation Shylock: A Confession* (New York: Simon and Schuster, 1993), 274.

* "Th-th-th-three th-th-th-thous-s-s-sand ducats-s-s": *Operation Shylock*, 275. Roth echoes the account of Macklin's performance by Georg Christoph Lichtenberg, *Letters from England*, excerpted in *The Merchant of Venice: The New Variorum*, ed. Horace Howard Furness (Philadelphia: Lippincott, 1888), 374.

Page 159

* "The most authentic Jewish homeland": *Operation Shylock*, 32.
* "People will be jubilant": *Operation Shylock*, 45.

Page 160

* "Something concealed": *Operation Shylock*, 27.
* "A conventionally better-looking face": *Operation Shylock*, 71–72.

Page 161

* "Famously real and prestigious archetype": *Operation Shylock*, 115.
* "Uncohesive, disappointed": *Operation Shylock*, 191.
* "The kid who pisses in his pants": *Operation Shylock*, 116.
* "Genie of grievance": *Operation Shylock*, 74.

Page 162

* "I AM YOUR GOOD NAME": *Operation Shylock*, 87.
* "Weightless and incorporeal": *Operation Shylock*, 78.
* "Is this a brilliant creative disposition": *Operation Shylock*, 83, 199.

Page 163

* "*Turns their religion into schlock*": *Operation Shylock*, 157.
* "Laughing at him": *Operation Shylock*, 204.

Page 164

* "Whatever I thought or did was wrong": *Operation Shylock*, 306–7.
* "Wouldn't convince me of anything": *Operation Shylock*, 364.
* "I am Philip Roth": *Operation Shylock*, 32.

Page 165

* "Vigorous, healthy boy": *Operation Shylock*, 60.

Page 166

* "Instigated by the wish": *Operation Shylock*, 130–31.
* "Human, elastic, adaptable": *Operation Shylock*, 126.
* "Jews were victims": *Operation Shylock*, 132.
* "Out of the bank of the dead six million": *Operation Shylock*, 135.

Page 167

* "Someone aroused and decomposing": *Operation Shylock*, 122, 129, 152.
* "At the core of everything": *Operation Shylock*, 129.

Page 167 (continued)

* "Better for real things to be uncontrollable": *Operation Shylock*, 290.

* "Steal from him, spit at him": *Operation Shylock*, 58.

* "Woman forged by the commonplace": *Operation Shylock*, 237.

Page 168

* "A mosaic of smithereens": *Operation Shylock*, 109.

Page 169

* *Loshon hora*: *Operation Shylock*, 332, 334.

Index